AF413128

Paganism and Celtic Shamanism

A Guide to Norse Magic, Druidism, Runes, Symbols, and More

Free Bonus from Silvia Hill available for limited time

Hi Spirituality Lovers!

My name is Silvia Hill, and first off, I want to THANK YOU for reading my book.

Now you have a chance to join my exclusive spirituality email list so you can get the ebooks below for free as well as the potential to get more spirituality ebooks for free! Simply click the link below to join.

P.S. Remember that it's 100% free to join the list.

~~$27~~ FREE BONUSES

- 9 Types of Spirit Guides and How to Connect to Them
- How to Develop Your Intuition: 7 Secrets for Psychic Development and Tarot Reading
- Tarot Reading Secrets for Love, Career, and General Messages

Access your free bonuses here

https://livetolearn.lpages.co/paganism-and-celtic-shamanism-paperback/

Table of Contents

Part 1: Paganism for Beginners

Unlocking Norse Magic, Druidry, Celtic Shamanism, Runes, Signs, and Symbols

Introduction

Most people think of Paganism as a single religion based on ancient healing traditions and reverence towards nature and polytheism. While it's true that both ancient and contemporary Pagan practices involve elements of healing, spirituality, nature, and the divine, there are many different approaches through which this is done. Even in ancient times, the number of Pagan religions was vast - and this was before they started to incorporate elements from other, more dominant religions like Christianity. In modern times, there is no limit to what you can incorporate into your practices. It's all about what feels right for you based on your cultural and religious background.

Polytheism and pantheism are still traditionally present in contemporary Pagan practices, as both beliefs allow for immense diversity. Whether you wish to honor one deity or several, it's totally up to you. Unlike in many other religions, female deities have just as distinguished roles as their male counterparts - and in some traditions, even more important ones.

Another factor that puts modern Pagan traditions apart from other religions and even ancient traditions is the choice of solitary practice. In ancient times, lone practitioners were rare to find. However, nowadays, due to the diversity of traditions, many people feel safe and confident learning the Pagan ways on their own. Whether you go down this path or want to join a coven, a group, or any other Pagan community, you'll have plenty of support from fellow practitioners.

Despite having different approaches, the names of some modern practices like Paganism and Wicca are used interchangeably. Wicca is one of the most popular Pagan practices nowadays - mainly because it's also the newest. This book will clarify all the differences between these two practices and lead you to the magical path of practical Wicca.

Other Pagan practices, such as Norse Paganism, can be just as inspiring. It's enough to delve into the tales of Nordic mythology to see how much these practices meant to the old Norse people. From guiding them through battles to protection during the harsh winters, Norse people relied on their gods and ancestors for everything. Their most common practice - runic divination- is still in use today. With the help of the information you'll receive in this book and enough spiritual dedication, you can learn this magical art too.

Another popular form of gathering wisdom in Norse Paganism was journeying. This was typically performed by shamans, who used the information they accessed for healing - whether physical, mental, or spiritual. However, as you'll learn from the book, Shamanism was also present in other Celtic Pagan approaches. Celtic Shamanism incorporates some of the most complex traditions, with some of them taking rigorous practice to master.

The book will also introduce you to Druidry - a practice shrouded in mysticism and only taught to selected members of society. In ancient times, Druids were the most (and sometimes only) educated members of Celtic tribes who recorded the tribe's history. While there are many ways to become a Druid, there are still plenty of mysteries around this practice. The lack of written evidence on ancient Druidry caused modern traditions to be loosely based on its ancestor.

Chapter 1: A Brief History of Paganism

Paganism is one of the oldest spiritual traditions in the world. It dates back to prehistoric times and can be found in many different cultures around the globe. Paganism is an umbrella term used to describe various earth-based spiritual traditions. It generally refers to a nature-based religion that worships and respects the earth and its creatures. It is often seen as a more ancient or primal form of religion, one that is closer to the natural world. Pagans believe that the divine can be found in all things and often look to nature for guidance and inspiration. Pagans often practice their faith through rituals and ceremonies that honor the earth and all its elements.

Paganism is one of the oldest spiritual traditions in the world.
https://www.pexels.com/photo/bottles-on-black-round-table-in-the-room-with-fireplace-and-cow-skull-7190305/

Paganism dates back thousands of years, and its origins can be traced back to some of the earliest known civilizations. Over the centuries, it has evolved and changed to reflect the cultures and beliefs of its practitioners. Today, there are many different forms of Paganism practiced all over the world.

The Origin of Paganism

Paganism is thought to have originated in the Stone Age with the early hunter-gatherer societies. This was the time when humans first began to form organized religions. Pagan beliefs and practices likely developed out of a need to explain the natural world and our place within it. As early humans began to domesticate plants and animals, they likely also began to develop a belief in animism, the idea that all living things have a spirit. This belief helped early humans to form a connection with the natural world and to understand its place within it. Pagan beliefs likely developed in small, tight-knit communities where everyone knew and trusted one another. As these communities grew more extensive and more complex, they began to develop organized religions.

Pagan beliefs likely first developed in Europe and Asia, as these were the regions where humans began forming organized religions. However, Paganism can be found in almost every culture across the globe.

Paganism can be traced back to various ancient cultures, such as the Celts, Greeks, and Romans. However, during the Middle Ages, Paganism began to take hold in Europe. This was due mainly to the Christianization of the continent. Christianity began to replace many of the older Pagan traditions. Still, some people continued to practice their Pagan beliefs in secret. This often led to persecution from the Church. In some cases, Pagans were even put to death for their beliefs.

Despite centuries of persecution, Paganism has survived and even thrived in many parts of the world. Today, there are an estimated two million Pagans worldwide.

Etymology

Paganism has its roots in pre-Christian, indigenous beliefs from around the world. The word "pagan" is derived from Latin and was likely used as a derogatory term by early Christians to describe those who continued to practice their Pagan beliefs. Over time, the term has been reclaimed by many Pagans and is now used proudly to describe themselves.

It was first used to describe people who did not follow the major world religions, such as Christianity, Judaism, and Islam. Over time, the word came to be associated with any religion that was not Christian.

It was widely practiced all over Europe, but with the rise of Christianity in the 4th century, it started declining. However, it was still practiced until the 10th century to some extent. In the 1500s, the Renaissance was a period of intense interest in classical culture; Paganism was incorporated into Europe's arts, music, literature, and ethics during this time.

Paganism began to re-emerge as a distinct religious movement in the 20th century. In the United Kingdom, the Pagan Federation was founded in 1971 to support Pagans of all traditions. Since then, the movement has grown steadily throughout the world.

Paganism is an umbrella term that covers a wide range of spiritual and religious beliefs. Some people use the term to describe their spirituality, while others refer to organized religions like Wicca, Druidry, and Heathenry.

What Is Paganism?

Paganism is a diverse and decentralized religious movement that centers on worshipping nature gods and goddesses. Pagans often celebrate their beliefs through rituals and festivals that honor the changing seasons and life cycles. Many Pagans also choose to live in harmony with the natural world, working to protect the environment from harm.

Paganism is not a single religion but a collection of different spiritual traditions. Some worship a specific god or goddess, while others focus on a group of deities.

Pagans also believe in magical and supernatural powers and benefit from spells and charms in their daily lives. Paganism has no central authority or figurehead, and there is no one set of beliefs or practices that all practitioners follow. Instead, each Pagan chooses what to believe and how to worship.

Pagan Gods

Paganism is a polytheistic religion that believes in multiple gods and goddesses. Each god or goddess represents a different aspect of the natural world or human experience. For example, there might be a god of the sun, a god of love, or a goddess of wisdom. Pagans also believe in magic and the power of nature.

Thor, Odin, Freyja, Frigg, Freyr, Tyr, Loki, and Heimall are the most well-known Norse deities. However, there were many lesser-known gods and goddesses. The pantheon of the Greek Olympians includes Zeus, Poseidon, Hades, Aphrodite, Hermes, and a host of other deities. Every aspect of human experience was attributed to one or more of these gods and goddesses.

Pagan Symbols

There are many misconceptions about Paganism, such as the idea that pagans worship the devil or that they are all witches. That is not accurate. Pagans do not believe in the devil, and not all of them are witches.

Some popular pagan symbols include the pentacle (a five-pointed star), the Celtic cross, the triple goddess, and the horned god. These symbols are often used in rituals, ceremonies, and everyday life. They are worn as jewelry, displayed on walls or altars, or carried in pockets or bags.

Paganism puts great stress on nature and the earth. It is often considered a form of animism, which is the belief that everything, including animals, plants, and rocks, has a spirit.

In the Egyptian pantheon, Isis and Osiris were the most popular gods. Isis was the goddess of motherhood and nature, while Osiris was the god of the underworld and the afterlife. Other popular Egyptian deities include Ra, the sun god, and Hathor, the goddess of love and beauty. The Roman pantheon includes Jupiter, the king of the gods, and Juno, the goddess of marriage and motherhood.

Pagan Beliefs and Rituals

Pagans believe in magic, reincarnation, karma, and the power of nature. Their rituals and celebrations are often based on the changing of the seasons and the cycles of nature. The most well-known Pagan festival is Beltane, celebrated on May 1st. Other popular Pagan festivals include Samhain (pronounced "sow-in"), celebrated on October 31st, and Imbolc, celebrated on February 2nd.

You'll find more information on the different beliefs and practices among different Pagan traditions later in this book. For now, let's take a closer look at the history of Paganism.

Paganism in Europe

European Paganism is a rich and varied belief system rooted in the ancient world. From the Celts to the Norse, pagans have long been associated with nature worship, magic, and deep respect for the natural world.

Pre-Christian Europe was a very different place than it is today. The land was mostly forest, and people lived in small villages or tribes. They were farmers or herders and worshipped gods and goddesses related to nature. There were many different tribes, each one with unique customs and beliefs.

When the Romans conquered Europe, they brought their religion, Christianity, with them. Christian missionaries tried to convert the pagans, but many held on to their old beliefs. Christianity gradually became the dominant religion, but Paganism never entirely died out. In the Middle Ages, there was a revival of Paganism in Europe, which has continued to grow.

Paganism in England

England has a long history of Paganism, dating back to the Bronze Age. The most well-known pagan deity in England is the goddess Brigid, the Lady of the Lake. She is associated with fire, healing, and poetry. Another popular deity is the Horned God, associated with hunting and animals.

The native tribes of England worshipped various gods and goddesses, including the god of the sun, the god of the moon, and the goddess of fertility. Paganism was the dominant religion in England until the arrival of Christianity in the 7th century.

Paganism declined during the 10th and 11th centuries as the Christian church became more powerful. By the 13th century, it had all but disappeared from England. However, it experienced a resurgence in the 18th and 19th centuries when people began to explore other religions.

Paganism in America

American Paganism has a long and complicated history. It is difficult to say precisely when or how Paganism first arrived on the shores of the United States. Some Pagans believe that the ancient indigenous peoples of North and South America practiced a form of it, while others believe that the first Pagans in America were European immigrants who brought their own beliefs and practices with them.

European colonists brought various pagan traditions, including Druidry, Celtic Shamanism, Norse Magic, and Wicca, to the Americas. These traditions mixed and mingled with each other and the native beliefs already present in America, creating a rich and diverse Pagan tradition.

Paganism continued to grow in popularity throughout the 19th and 20th centuries. In the 1960s and 1970s, the feminist and civil rights movements sparked a renewed interest in Paganism and other alternative spiritualities. In the late 20th century, Paganism began to regain popularity in America. This resurgence was partly due to the growing awareness of environmental issues and the popularity of books and movies that featured pagan characters (such as The Lord of the Rings and Harry Potter).

Today, there are an estimated 1 million Pagans in America, and the number is increasing daily.

History of Paganism in Iceland

Paganism was the dominant religion in Iceland before the Christianization of the island in 1000 AD. It is thought that Paganism first arrived in Iceland around 900 AD, brought by settlers from Scandinavia and the British Isles. Paganism continued to be practiced in Iceland even after Christianity became the dominant religion.

Iceland did not officially become a Christian country until 1000CE. Paganism declined in popularity after that, but some Icelanders still practiced it into the 13th century. After that, Christianity became the only religion practiced in Iceland.

The Icelandic Pagans also believed in many other beings, such as elves, dwarves, giants, and trolls. Some of these beings were thought to be helpful, while others were considered to be dangerous. Pagan beliefs and practices were passed down orally from generation to generation.

There are no written records of Paganism in Iceland, so we know about it mostly from Christian sources written after the country converted to Christianity.

Norway and Sweden

Paganism was also the dominant religion in Norway and Sweden before Christianization. The pagan religion held out longest in northern lands, Norway and Sweden.

Norway had an early start in its conversion to Christianity, with King Haakon I (ruled 934-961 C.E.) accepting that religion in the 1020s. The country was, however, slow to give up its pagan ways. It was not until the early 11th century that Christianity became firmly established in Norway.

Sweden, on the other hand, did not accept Christianity until the middle of the 11th century. King Olof Skötkonung (ruled 995-1022 C.E.) was the first Swedish ruler to be baptized in 1001 C.E., but it was not until his son, Anund Jakob (ruled 1008-1050 C.E.), that Christianity became widely accepted in Sweden.

Paganism in Asia

Paganism is also practiced in many parts of Asia. In Japan, the native religion, Shinto, is a form of Paganism. Many Pagans in China practice Taoism, an indigenous Chinese religion with elements of Paganism.

In India, there are numerous pagan traditions still practiced today. And in Korea, Shamanism is still practiced by a small minority of the population.

Paganism in Ireland

Ireland was a pagan country before the arrival of Christianity in the 5th century. Pagans in Ireland continue to practice a variety of ancient traditions. These traditions include the construction of temporary altars or shrines, the lighting of fires, and the offering of gifts to the gods and goddesses. They also celebrate various seasonal festivals, such as Beltane and Mabon.

Neo-Paganism in Ireland is a modern movement that revives ancient pagan traditions. It is practiced by a small minority of people in Ireland, most of whom are members of the Pagan Federation of Ireland. There are several different types of Neo-Paganism practiced in Ireland.

Paganism in Africa

It is often associated with ancient Egyptian religion and, more recently, with the traditional religions of the San people. However, there is no one African Pagan tradition. Instead, there are a variety of pagan traditions that are followed across the continent.

African traditions believe that ancestors maintain spiritual connections with living relatives. There is a general tendency for ancestral spirits to be kind and good. Negative actions by ancestral spirits cause minor illnesses and warn people that they have crossed the wrong path.

San people, also known as Bushmen, are indigenous people of Southern Africa. The San follow a pagan religion based on animism, the belief that everything in nature has a spirit. Ancestors are thought to be powerful spirits who can help or harm the living.

Australia and New Zealand

Paganism is also practiced in Australia and New Zealand. The most common type of Paganism in these countries is Wicca.

The pagan religion of the Māori people is known as the Māori religion. As a form of animism, it holds that everything in nature is spiritual. Māori religion teaches that humans are connected to all things in nature and that we must respect and care for the natural world.

Paganism is a growing religion in Australia. In 2016, it was estimated that there were about 27194 Pagans in Australia. This number is expected to grow in the future.

Paganism and the Indian Sub-Continent

Paganism was also practiced in the Indian subcontinent. The most common type of Paganism in the sub-continent is Hinduism. It is the oldest and most prominent religion in the sub-continent. It is a polytheistic religion, meaning Hindus believe in many gods and goddesses. There are millions of Hindus living in the sub-continent.

Paganism Today

This is a hard number to estimate because Paganism is not an organized religion like Christianity. There is no single Pagan organization or leader. Instead, Paganism is a collection of many different spiritual and religious traditions. Each tradition has its own beliefs, practices, and followers.

It is believed that there are between 1 and 4 million Pagans worldwide. Most Pagans live in the United States, followed by the United Kingdom, Canada, and Australia.

Misconception about Paganism

Paganism is often misunderstood and misrepresented by mainstream society, largely because Pagans do not have a central authority or figurehead, such as the Pope in Catholicism. As a result, Paganism is often seen as an amorphous and disorganized religion. Additionally, Paganism has no strict dogma or creed, which further contributes to its misunderstood reputation.

Paganism is also frequently associated with Satanism because both religions share similar beliefs and practices. However, Pagans do not worship Satan or any other malevolent deity. Instead, they believe in a pantheon of gods and goddesses who represent various aspects of the natural world.

Paganism is not an evil or dark religion. In fact, Pagans have a deep respect for nature and all living things. They believe that we are all connected to the earth and its elements. It is a peaceful and tolerant religion that celebrates life in all its forms.

The roots of Paganism can be traced back to the ancient civilizations of Mesopotamia, Egypt, and Greece. These cultures all believed in a pantheon of gods and goddesses who ruled over the natural world. They also shared other similarities, such as a belief in magic and the use of oracles and divination.

Types of Paganism

There are many different types of Paganism. Some of the most common types include Animism, Druidism, Wicca, Odinism, Asatru, Celtic Reconstructionism, and Heathenry. As an umbrella term, Paganism refers to various spiritual and religious beliefs. Each type has its own set of beliefs and practices.

Animism is the belief that everything in nature has a spirit. This includes animals, plants, rocks, and even inanimate objects. Animism is one of the oldest religions in the world.

Druidism is a type of Paganism that honors the gods and goddesses of Celtic mythology. Druids were the priestly class of the Celts. They were responsible for performing ceremonies, such as weddings and funerals. Druidism is a nature-based religion that emphasizes harmony with the natural world.

Wicca is a type of Paganism that worships the goddesses of nature. Wiccans believe in magic and the power of spells and rituals. Having been founded in the 1950s, Wicca is still a relatively new religion.

Odinism is a type of Paganism that revolves around worshiping the Norse gods, like Odin and Thor. Odinists believe in the power of magic and runes. They also place great importance on courage, honor, and loyalty.

Asatru is a type of Paganism that worships the Norse gods. Asatru is similar to Odinism, but it emphasizes ethics and morality more.

Celtic Reconstructionism is a type of Paganism that seeks to revive the Celtic culture and religion. Celtic Reconstructionists believe in following the old ways of their ancestors. They also place great importance on preserving the Celtic language and culture.

Heathenry is a type of Paganism that worships the Germanic gods, such as Odin and Thor. Heathens believe in magic and the power of runes. They also place great importance on courage, honor, and loyalty.

The following chapters will introduce you to some of the most common beliefs of Paganism. You'll learn about their practices. By the end of this book, you'll have a good understanding of the different types of Paganism and how they differ.

Paganism is an ancient and varied religious tradition emphasizing nature worship, personal autonomy, and individual spiritual experience. Paganism first emerged in the early days of human civilization, when people began to worship the natural world around them. This early form of religion focused on animism, or the belief that everything in nature contains a spirit.

As societies developed, Paganism evolved to include the worship of specific deities associated with different aspects of nature. This led to the rise of polytheistic pagan religions, which worship multiple gods and goddesses. Paganism also began to incorporate mystical practices like magic and divination. These elements were often seen as ways to connect with the divine or natural world.

In recent years, Paganism has experienced a resurgence in popularity, particularly in the form of Neo-Paganism. This modern pagan movement emphasizes a return to nature worship and pagan values.

Chapter 2: Pagan Beliefs and Spirituality

Paganism isn't just a belief but also a spiritual concept. Unlike many other beliefs that mainly focus on sinning, punishment, and suffering, the ancient pagans had a more positive view of the world. They regarded it as a place to live life to the fullest and experience happiness and joy. The pagans believed that the divine was always around them in everything that nature embodies. They often felt close to the divine and one with the universe, which is why nature is highly revered in Paganism.

The pagans believed that the divine was always around them in everything that nature embodies

https://www.pexels.com/photo/ornaments-and-lighted-candle-on-a-table-6154151/

This chapter will delve into Paganism as a spiritual concept and further discuss its various deities, beliefs, festivals, and the significance of nature in Paganism.

The Ancient Pagans' Beliefs

Ancient Paganism revolved around polytheism which is the belief in the existence and the worshiping of multiple deities. Unlike monotheists, who believe there is only one god who is responsible for everything, polytheists believe there is a different god for every aspect of life. The ancient pagans even believed that there were different deities for cities, forests, families, streams, and mountains.

Paganism is more flexible and welcoming than other beliefs and religions due to how inclusive polytheism is. If you look at any monotheistic religion, you'll find that they are all exclusive. For instance, Christians don't practice Judaism or go to temples, and vice versa. If one chooses to practice a religion, one must stick to it, as followers of monotheistic religions aren't allowed to practice more than one religion. The ancient pagans didn't have to follow these strict rules. Since they were polytheists, they were free to worship as many gods as they wanted. This made Paganism one of the most tolerant and diverse beliefs. Pagans believed they could worship any deity they wanted and still be accepted without any judgment.

The pagans worshiped both male and female deities, and these gods and goddesses were depicted as regular human beings. They weren't perfect. They were flawed like the rest of mankind. Yet, they were highly revered for their power and wisdom.

Although many religions believe in the afterlife and that all their actions heavily influence what their life will be like in the afterlife, pagans have a different view. They didn't concern themselves with what will happen after death and only focused on their lives instead. In fact, some pagans didn't believe in the existence of the afterlife or any similar concept to heaven and hell. However, their ancient literary works told a different story as many of their classics featured the idea of the afterlife, like in the famous poem Odyssey by Homer. This poem, and other similar literary works, were entertaining and even masterpieces, but they didn't always provide an actual portrayal of the ancient pagans' beliefs. Their remaining tombstones showed their lack of belief in the afterlife. They often inscribed Latin abbreviations on their tombstones to indicate that the deceased doesn't exist anymore. This proves that they believe the soul ceased to exist after death. As a result, some pagans didn't live their lives to please their gods. They didn't believe there was such a thing as sinning, so they didn't feel the need to atone for their mistakes, repent, or ask for salvation. They believed in being good individuals because it gave them a sense of pride and fulfillment and didn't involve the afterlife or pleasing their deities.

However, this wasn't the case for all pagans, as others firmly believed in the afterlife and lived their lives according to a set of rules in the hopes that their souls would end up in a better place after they died. For instance, the Vikings and Norse people believed in the afterlife and had a similar concept of heaven that they called Valhalla, a place where the souls of noble warriors go after they die. The ancient Greeks believed that the soul traveled to the underworld, which was ruled by the god Hades, where they would spend eternity. The ancient Egyptians also believed in the afterlife and that death wasn't the end of the soul's journey. In fact, death transitions the soul from the realm of the living to the realm of the dead. Where and how they would spend their afterlife depended on how they lived their lives. Just like some people nowadays believe that good people go to heaven while bad ones go to hell, the pagans had similar beliefs. Those who led an honorable life ended up in the Field of Reeds, their version of heaven, where good people spent their afterlife. However, if a person committed many bad deeds and lived dishonorable lives, they would be severely punished, and their soul would cease to exist.

Pagans also believed in karma, defined in the modern world as "what goes around, comes around." In other words, your actions will impact your destiny, whether good or bad. It isn't the gods or even the concept of fate that is responsible for karma; it is a law of life that many people today believe and live by. Reincarnation was another belief in ancient Paganism that was associated with karma. It is believed that when the body withers after a person dies, the soul can experience a rebirth, whether in the form of a human being, animal, or plant. What or who you come back to depends on your karma. Although few pagans believed in reincarnation, there were a number of them that accepted this belief. Some religions and beliefs don't have a favorable outlook on reincarnation; however, the pagans' view was more positive. They considered it a joyful experience where the soul could learn and grow.

Ancient Paganism and the Myth of Creation

How was the world created? This is a question that many religions and beliefs have attempted to answer, and Paganism is no different. According to many religions, there is God, and He is the one who created the universe.

While others believe that the universe was the result of the big bang theory, the answer to this question is Paganism may be tricky. There are different beliefs in Paganism, and each has its own myth of how the world came to be. However, most of the creation stories in this belief share the same elements. The first element is that before mankind came to be, there was nothing, an emptiness, and the world was chaotic and dark. This darkness was different from the normal darkness that mankind is accustomed to when the sun sets. It was the original darkness that was impossible to imagine or comprehend. It was what the world looked like before order was established. The universe was created from the void, and everything that threatened the universe's order or caused chaos was sent to the underworld. Chaos was never destroyed but remained in the background threatening to rule over the world once again.

Order usually comes out of nothing; however, each story has its own interpretation of this moment. For instance, according to ancient Greek mythology, the world came to be through birth. The void, an all-goddess called Eurynome, mated with a serpent called Ophion, who was also a void and gave birth to the universe. In ancient Egyptian mythology, the universe came to be through the God Ptah masturbating. These myths and others have in common that a certain action took place to create the universe, which is the second common element that all creation myths share.

The third element that creation myths have in common is that mankind was created in the creator's image, and the universe and all its beings represent this creator. This means that all creation is planned, and nothing is done by accident. In other words, what the deity creates is a mirror of them and their nature.

The Ancient Pagan's Deities

The ancient pagans assigned a deity for everything. This makes sense since they didn't have the methods that exist in the modern world, like technology, modern medicine, or irrigation methods. Everything seemed out of their control, so they wanted to rely on something more powerful and wiser than themselves. These deities came through where mankind failed. They made their lives easier and, in some cases, better. These deities could take away their misery and pain and provide for the people.

Now, we will look at the most significant deities in ancient Paganism.

Odin

If you are familiar with Marvel comics and the Thor movies, then the name Odin will definitely ring a bell. He was the chief deity in Norse mythology and the god of war, poetry, and wisdom. Odin lived in Valhalla and had shape-shifting abilities. He would often change his form and walk among mankind. Although Odin is often depicted as an old man with one eye, this isn't his original form. He used to have two eyes, but he exchanged one of them to gain immense wisdom. Odin had an eight-legged horse named Sleipnir that he rode over the water and across the skies.

Thor

Almost everyone is familiar with Thor, thanks to comic books that made this deity very popular. Thor is Odin's son, one of the most significant deities in Norse mythology. He was the god of thunder, lightning, and fertility. Thor was known for his strength which is why he was the guardian of Asgard. Asgard is the realm where many Norse deities reside. Thor's weapon, Mjollnir, was a huge and powerful hammer. It was dwarves that made Mjollnir for Thor, and he used it against powerful evil creatures like snakes and giants. Thor is often depicted as a bearded man with red hair. Although most people associate Thor with thunder, he also played a huge role in agriculture. People often presented offerings to Thor during times of drought so he would bless them with rain.

Loki

Forget everything you have learned about Loki from the movies because his role in Norse mythology is different and smaller than that of Odin and Thor. Loki was a demi-god and Thor's brother. He was the god of mischief, trickery, and fire. He wasn't a deity that people worshiped or revered, as he didn't provide any help or bestow any blessings. Loki thrived on chaos; his main purpose was to play tricks and cause trouble for deities and mankind. There was no deeper meaning for his actions; everything he did was for his own enjoyment. Like Odin, Loki also had shapeshifting abilities and could transform into a man, a woman, or any type of animal.

Frigga

Frigga, or Frigg, was Odin's wife and was often referred to as the Queen of Heaven. She was the mother to three of Odin's sons: Hermod, Baldur, and Höðr. She was the goddess of marriage and fertility and could see the future. Frigga was very wise and intelligent, even wiser than Odin himself. There is a beautiful meaning behind Frigga's name. It is derived from the Norse word fríja, which translates to "to love." Have you ever wondered why many people prefer to get married on Fridays? This is meant to honor Frigga, who this day was named after her.

Heimdall

Heimdall was Thor's son, and he was the god of light. He had the gift of prophecy and was able to see the future. His senses were sharper than many other gods. He could hear everything around him, even in the far distance. He also could see for hundreds of miles, whether day or night. He is often depicted with a gold tooth. He guarded the Bifrost Bridge, the bridge (path) between Asgard and Earth. Heimdall plays a very prominent role in Norse mythology as he guarded all the gods in Asgard, and he is the one that will warn them when Ragnarok (the end of the world) occurs. He is believed to blow on a magical horn that would alert all of Asgard that the end of the world is here.

Zeus

Shifting from Norse deities to Greek ones. Since he was the king of all gods, Zeus was the most significant god in Greek mythology. Zeus killed his father, Kronos, and became the supreme deity and lived on Mount Olympus. He married his sister Hera, the goddess of marriage. Zeus was a very powerful god responsible for everything in the universe, like time, fate, order, and the weather. As a result, he was highly revered among the ancient Greeks.

Poseidon

Poseidon was the Greek god of the seas, horses, storms, and earthquakes. He is often depicted holding a trident with a dolphin by his side. Like the seas he ruled over, Poseidon's temper was unpredictable. He could experience moments of peace and tranquility; at other times, he could be violent and angry like a storm.

Minerva

Minerva was the Roman goddess of arts and wisdom, similar to her Greek counterpart Athena. She was the daughter of Jupiter, the chief deity in ancient Rome. However, Jupiter swallowed Minerva's mother, Metis, when she was pregnant with her because there was a prophecy that this child would be stronger than he ever was. When inside Jupiter, Metis created armor and made weapons for her daughter, which Minerva used to make so much noise. Jupiter couldn't handle the noise, so he split his own head open, and Minerva was born from it.

The Significance of Nature in Ancient Paganism

Nature was highly revered in ancient Paganism. The ancient pagans believed they could recognize the divine in nature. They regarded nature as something sacred. Birth, life, and death were more than just cycles that every person must experience; they carried deep spiritual meaning. Mankind didn't hold any significance over other creatures or natural objects. They were equal to animals, plants, trees, etc. However, it is essential to note that pagans didn't worship nature but only held it in high regard because they believed that the divine was everywhere.

Ancient Pagan Festivals

Every belief has its own festivities where its followers either celebrate a deity or a change in the seasons, and Paganism is no different. Here, we will cover some of the most popular ancient pagan festivals, many of which pagans celebrate to this day.

Samhain

Samhain took place on the Celtic new year, which was October 31. Halloween is also a popular festival that takes place on this date. In fact, modern-day Halloween was heavily influenced by the celebrations of Samhain. The word "Samhain" means summer's end, and it celebrates the end of the harvest season and the beginning of the dark and cold weather. Samhain was a very special time for the Celts as it allowed them to connect with their ancestors. They believed an invisible veil separated the physical world from the other world. This veil was at its weakest during Samhain, which allowed the spirits of the dead to travel between worlds. Besides the spirits of the dead, ghosts, fairies, and demons were all free to visit this realm.

Saturnalia

Saturnalia was an ancient Roman festival that celebrated the winter solstice. As the name indicates, this festival celebrated the Roman god of agriculture, Saturn. Similar to Halloween, Christmas was also heavily influenced by Saturnalia. The festival occurred in early December and often lasted for a week. During this festival, the ancient Romans lived a life of extreme pleasure and did everything in excess. Just like Christmas traditions, people ate, drank, and exchanged gifts.

Yule

Yule was a Celtic festival that took place in mid-winter. This is the time of year when the days would begin to be longer, and this festival celebrates the return of the sun. People celebrated this festival by drinking, exchanging stories, and lighting bonfires. They also burned Yule logs for twelve days so its light could vanquish evil spirits that appear on the dark days of winter. Christmas has also borrowed many of its traditions from this festival.

Imbolc

Imbolc was a Celtic festival that took place on February 1st and second. This festival occurs after the winter solstice and before the spring equinox in various places around Europe. Pagans revered and celebrated the goddess of arts and crafts, Brigid, on this day.

Akitu

Akitu was a Babylonian festival that celebrated the beginning of spring. The festival revolved around the story of the marriage between the Babylonian chief god Marduk and the goddess of the Earth, Ishtar. According to the story, Marduk traveled to marry his bride Ishtar at night. During Akitu, the ancient Babylonians celebrated the union between heaven and the earth, just like the one between Marduk and Ishtar.

Wepet Renpet

Wepet Renpet was an ancient Egyptian festival, and it was celebrated on the ancient Egyptian new year, which took place on September 11th on the Gregorian calendar. However, the date of this festival wasn't fixed as it mainly depended on the flow of Egypt's most significant river, the Nile. The festival also celebrated the death and resurrection of Osiris, the god of agriculture, fertility, resurrection, and the afterlife. Osiris was murdered by his brother Seth, but his devoted wife Isis found him and brought him back to life, where he then became the god of the dead and the underworld. Wepet Renpet was one of the most popular festivals in ancient Egypt since Osiris had many followers at the time.

As you may have noticed, almost all pagan festivals involve the beginning, end, or a prominent time in each season. Most pagans' festivals usually mark a specific time during the seasons, which shows how significant of a role the four seasons played in their celebrations.

Paganism focused on the worship of many deities and allowed people to worship as many gods as they wanted. Their deities played a significant role in their lives as the people assigned a god to every aspect of their lives to protect them and provide help when all earthly methods failed. Nature, gods, and festivals all played a huge role in Paganism and helped influence many neo-pagan beliefs.

Chapter 3: Neopaganism vs. Wicca

As is the natural course of traditions, Paganism as a religion has evolved. The way it's practiced in modern times is often very different from the ancient customs. Due to the diversity of the followers' needs, more branches became available, and many other religions have left their mark on Pagan practices. These belief systems are classified under an umbrella term called Neopaganism. One of the most widely recognized branches of Neopaganism is Wicca, which is one of the newest forms of Pagan spiritual practices. Seeing how both draw inspiration from ancient pagan traditions, including the festivities, rituals, and more, *Neopaganism* and *Wicca* are often mistakenly used interchangeably. The similar cultural references in modern media and pop culture don't help dispel the confusion. However, as you'll see from this chapter, the two are entirely separate religions. Not only are their definitions different, but they often have different approaches to their practices.

One of the most widely recognized branches of Neopaganism is Wicca.
https://www.pexels.com/photo/man-people-woman-art-7190312/

Are Neopagans and Wiccans the Same?

One of the reasons Neopaganism and Wicca are often depicted as one and the same is that almost all Wicca practitioners are Neopagans - at least to a certain degree. However, not all Neopagans are Wiccans because many choose to follow different paths that have nothing to do with what modern Wicca stands for. To make things more confusing, not all Wiccans practice their craft similarly. Some will openly embrace witchcraft - while others choose to leave magic out of their practices. Others practice magic without embarking on a pagan path. Instead, they remain faithful to religions that marked their past because they feel they align with their values more. Whichever course one takes is a highly personal choice each practitioner can make on their own accord. The beauty of spirituality-based religions is that when following them, you're free to act in whichever way feels right to you. If you have trouble understanding the difference between the two approaches, the rest of this chapter will help clarify things. It can be a great stepping stone if you decide to embrace the Wiccan path - with or without magic.

What Is Neopaganism?

Neopaganism is defined as a collective term for several types of spirituality - which are more or less based on ancient pagan traditions. Some of the most popular Pagan belief systems practiced today are Asatru, Thelema, Druidism, Heathenry, Shamanism, Animism, and Reconstructionism. There are also Pagans who don't follow any specific religion. They try to adopt the ancient Celtic Pagan traditions of relying on nature for sustenance, guidance, and spiritual growth.

Originating from centuries-old Paganism, Neopaganism has emerged as a way to bring forward religions based on pre-Christian beliefs throughout Europe. It started as a byproduct of the counterculture spreading through North America during the 1960s. At that time, it was primarily based on environmentally conscious beliefs and equality expressed in new, creative ways. While inspired by the ancient Pagan traditions, it was presented to people in a way they needed it. This trend has continued in our now technologically advanced world, where there is even more need for finding a connection with nature. Since Neopaganism is not a centralized religion, the number of ways one can express Neopagan beliefs is nearly limitless. Most practitioners work alone throughout the year and gather during festivities during the equinoxes and other sabbats. Despite meeting only a handful of times a year, most Neopagans are incredibly supportive of each other's practices and have similar values.

Life-affirming is one of the qualities all Neopagans hold in high regard, regardless of their branch and any other beliefs they might have. They acknowledge that life has a beginning, a middle, and an end. Death, like in nature, is just a part of human life. It often comes with pain in suffering, but that's just the way things go in the natural world. For that reason, instead of fearing the dark days that come before death, many Neopagans seek wisdom and peace in the late stages of their lives. They also revere this stage because, for them, the purpose of life is found in the present existence and not after it. They live in the moment because they know they can learn from each experience. Difficulties are viewed as opportunities and not as punishment.

Similarly to their ancestors, the Pagans of today are typically either polytheistic or eventually duotheistic, meaning the followers worship several or at least two deities. Neopagans may even worship modern gods or choose to make new interpretations of the ancient ones. The archetypes of the Horned God, the Triple Moon Goddess, or the Dying God are still present. However, some practitioners will refer to the divine feminine as the Great Goddess of the Earth, Gaia. Male deities may also be called different names that complement their female counterparts.

For Neopagans, the divine power often transcends gender - which is yet another powerful reason for the resurgence of this religion. Some deities have both male and female elements - and even those with only one aspect are held in high esteem, regardless of gender. This allows practitioners to honor their male and female deities through the same traditions and practices. It also enables women to practice their religion the same way men do. For Neopagans, the image of the Goddess represents change - and her power is evidenced in nature. The cyclical shifts of feminine power that creates life, nurture it, and die afterward are also honored in this religion. This reverence is reflected in the movement of the celestial bodies, the seasons, and the life cycle of living beings. Pantheism is also a common belief among Neopagans. They believe that people have divine qualities - and when they reach for divine wisdom, they have to look inside and not outside themselves. Instead of looking for higher power, they practice delving deeper into their subconscious. Because, once again, power comes from nature, and it's inside everyone - and everyone can access it if they look deep enough into themselves. Others see gods as literal beings with specific needs and preferences.

Whether performed on special occasions or daily, the work of a Neopagan is always intentional. For example, celebrating the solar solstices and turning of the seasons is always done at the right time on what they call the "Wheel of the Year." In addition, they often create new rituals or tailor the old ones if they feel this helps them get better results. This often helps them enhance their experiences and allows them to connect with nature even more.

Another common element that defines Neopagans is the reverence of nature or the earth itself. Nature is sacred and everywhere, permeating everything with its essence - from humans to every other living being. This intrinsic value drives Neopagans to stay immersed in their environment, communicate with it, honor it, and stay true to it. Whether the practitioners work alone or belong to a community with whom they share their cultural beliefs, they'll try to remain as true to nature as possible. In today's world, people are often disconnected from nature, and one of the goals of contemporary pagans is to change that. They feel that the only way to save and honor the natural world is to express its sacredness and renew their connection with it. They often use the term "re-enchanting nature," which means nothing more than slowing down and allowing one to see just how precious the natural world is.

Neopaganism encompasses an incredibly eclectic and colorful set of practices. It embraces the teachings of ancient wisdom, the expression of new ideas, and everything in between. Just as there is diversity in nature, so are the different cultures and ideological beliefs. Neopagans honor this diversity and don't accept any form of intolerance and discrimination towards other ideas. No matter how firmly a practitioner stands in their beliefs, they'll always listen to what others say without prejudice or judgment. It may not work for them, but they see no reason why it couldn't work for others. According to Neopagans, everyone is free to decide what they believe in, and there is no absolute truth.

Apart from nature and life, Neopagans also hold their own bodies to be sacred. They use their body to communicate with the natural world, which means they rely on it on a regular basis. Because of this, they always strive to nourish and listen to its cues when something is wrong or needs to be changed in order to avoid an injury or illness. They allow themselves to enjoy everything that feels good for their bodies, from food to exercise to meditation - without guilt or the need to explain this to others.

What Is Wicca?

While Wicca is also an Earth-based religion, it has a slightly different approach to spiritual development. It relies primarily on magic to achieve this and many other specific goals. It was founded by Gerard Gardner in the late 1930s. After traveling through Asia and being fascinated by the different religions he encountered on his journey, Gardner arrived in England. There, he was introduced to a coven of Pagan practitioners who delved into witchcraft. Instead of embracing this practice as it is, Gardner formed a new one. He then incorporated elements from several other religions he was familiar with. This new religion was called Wicca, which means "witch" in Old English. Soon after it was founded, Wicca began to spread from England to Ireland, Scotland, and Wales. A couple of decades later, in the 1970s, it reached other continents, including North America. However, it took another decade until people started to view Wicca as a legitimate religion and not just a few people interested in the occult and Satanism.

Unlike traditional Neopagan beliefs, followers of Wicca rarely worship more than two deities. Because of this, the God and Goddess are often viewed as the only two deities you can ask for guidance. The male deity is also identified as Cerrunos, the Lord of Death, the Horned God, or the Leader of the Wild Hunt. Wiccan traditions with a closer connection to nature may also call him the Oak King or the Holly King - and honor him as such in festivals and ceremonies. The foremost Pagan female deity is the Triple Goddess. She has all three faces of a woman - the Maiden, the Mother, and the Crone. She may also bear the name of Aradia. Gardener's Wicca was only centered around one deity who could take on both male and female attributes. Although, according to Gardner, it didn't really matter whether it was male or female as long as people respected both when they worshipped.

Because Wicca is still loosely based on ancient Pagan traditions, it's not surprising that the deities they honor were all members of the Celtic pantheon. Of course, there are always exceptions to the rule. For example, some practitioners remain faithful to the gods from the religion they previously followed, despite embracing Paganism. There are also atheistic branches of contemporary Paganism - whose followers don't honor any deities.

Some Wiccans worship only one god or goddess. Whereas others honor several of them, calling on them for specific purposes. For example, there is a branch that emphasizes the role of feminine energies. Their followers only worship the Goddess and don't recognize male energy - deviating from the ancient Celtic Pagan customs. Honoring one deity is also common for those who converted from monotheistic religions like Christianity, which only acknowledges one god. Wiccans who convert from these religions often keep worshiping the same entity they worshiped before. They do it with the addition of higher spiritual goals and possibly magic.

Since Wicca is even named after the practitioners of witchcraft, it has become universally accepted that all Wiccans practice this art. However, this isn't always the case. Wiccans highly emphasize spiritual growth because it promotes the development of one's intuition. Wiccans use magic by connecting their energy to the energy contained in magical tools, elements of nature, and even inanimate objects. To do this, they must learn to rely on their intuition. They believe that the knowledge of how to harness magic is held in the subconscious - and the shortest way to access it is by listening to one's gut feelings. Once they gain access to magical energies, they'll know how to manipulate them to manifest the changes they want to make.

Wicca can be practiced in groups (or covens, as witches call them) or alone. One enters a coven after a brief induction period and remains as long as one chooses. Whether you wish to practice alone or in a coven, you can incorporate several different ideas into your practice. Some of the common branches of modern Wicca are Celtic, Eclectic, Faerie, Gardnerian (or original as it is the one based on Gardner's ideas), and Ceremonial Magic. All these originate from Paganism, but their founders have made sure to point out the distinction between their ideas and the traditional Pagan approach to life.

Witchcraft in Wicca can be used as a simple tool to harness magical energy without the practitioners adopting any spiritual beliefs. To practice witchcraft, you don't have to follow Pagan traditions like the reverence of nature, deities, or the life cycle. So, as you see, the connection between Neopaganism, Wicca, and witchcraft is much more complicated than how it's represented in mainstream media. Whichever path you choose is based on your personal preferences. However, there is a chance that you won't be able to avoid at least two of these three terms interfering with each other.

In Wicca, practitioners can choose how to interact with the deities, spiritual guides, and other entities they may rely on for guidance, healing, or magical help for various purposes. Some will freely interact with the deities, and they consider them quite approachable. Other Wiccans view the deities only as personifications of values and attributes they want to gain. They will aim to harness their wisdom through specific tools and not by communicating with a particular deity they need help from.

Another common element of all Wiccan approaches is the Wiccan Rede. This dictates that anything is permitted as long as it doesn't harm anyone. This is particularly significant because many Wiccans can distinguish between dark and light magic. Most will only work with light magic as they want to ensure that the way they manipulate energy won't harm anyone. Many advise that the first person to experience the negative effects is typically the practitioner themselves - forcing them to abide by the law of threefold return. According to Wicca, all of the practitioner's actions (good or bad) come back three times. Consequently, the triple effects would affect them the most, whether the act was aimed at them or someone else.

Wiccans show reverence for the four primordial elements of nature (air, fire, water, and earth). Traditionally, they tie these to a fifth element (the spirit). In their magical practices, Wiccans often associate the elements with the four states of matter (plasma, solid, gas, and liquid). Knowing which element controls which state allows them to infuse their tools with magical energy.

Besides the elements of nature, Wiccans also honor the seasons, similarly to how the Pagan ancestors did. According to them, each season represents the end of a significant period in people's lives and nature - and the beginning of another one. The veneration of the Horned God and the Triple Goddess of fertility also stems from these traditions. In addition, following the Western esotericism from which Wicca draws some of its ideas and basics, the religion promotes the need for spiritual development through its connection with nature and its magic. Even if not all practitioners rely on magic directly, they can still use it to spread good energy, peace, and love.

Are You a Neopagan, Wiccan, or Both?

If you're still unsure whether Wicca or any other form of Paganism is the right path for you to follow, the following quiz will help you decide:

- Do find grounding exercises enough to reconnect with nature?

- Do you feel the need to honor several deities and revere the change they bring to people's lives?

- Do you embrace life's cycle as a whole, even its dark side, knowing that it only leads to rebirth?

- Do you prefer general life-affirming practices over the ones that lead to specific goals with the help of specific tools?

- Do you identify yourself with the beliefs of Asatru, Heathenry, Druidism, or any other Pagan practice that doesn't rely on witchcraft?

- Do you prefer ancient techniques over modern approaches in Pagan practices?

If you answered most of these questions with yes, you are a Neopagan. You prefer following nature's rhythm and letting it guide you instead of relying on magical acts. If you answered most of the questions with no, you are a Wiccan. Magic is part of your life, and you feel it's helping you achieve your spiritual goals or anything else you desire. You are both if you have an almost equal number of yes and no answers. You are a Neopagan who embraces ancient traditions and combines them with the regular use of magic in their practices. You may not use magic daily, but you'll definitely reach for it if you really need to.

Chapter 4: Practical Wicca

Now that you've learned the background of Wicca, it's time for you to explore the practical side of it. In this chapter, you'll find hands-on advice on how to start your practice with the essentials like setting an altar, making a book of shadows, casting a protective circle, and more. Feel free to use the tools, methods, and spells you've given here, or create some of your own traditions with items you feel more aligned with.

Most Wiccan traditions recommend using a symbol for the god and the goddess.
https://www.pexels.com/photo/two-women-with-rings-in-black-jackets-touching-bull-skull-7189116/

Preparing for Work

Since Wiccan magic is so personal, you'll need to prepare yourself before any work (including the basics like setting up an altar). First, you'll need to cleanse your body and mind. You can do this by taking a cleansing bath, meditation, or even simple breathing exercises. Smudging is another excellent option for cleaning. You can use it to dispel negative energy from your sacred space and purify your body and senses. Apart from these preparation methods, you should always wash your hands before you do anything relating to magic. It's also a good idea to swipe the floors and air the room before you get to work.

Timing is crucial for magical practices. You can optimize your timing by choosing the right time of the day, week, or month when you start gathering supplies, decorating, and forming your intentions and spells. For example, you should think about setting an altar at sunset or after it under the moonlight - even if you're doing a simple one for daily practice. Decorations and certain tools should only be used at specific times, and using them at any other time may render them ineffective. It's also crucial to get your intention sorted out in time. Without a clear intent, you won't be able to focus your energy and reveal any wisdom you require for success. Ideally, you should coordinate forming your intention with the time you begin preparing the tools you use for every spell, ritual, and other magical act.

Creating an Altar

While having an altar isn't a prerequisite for successful magical work, it does help focus your energy and thoughts in the right direction. With a Wiccan practice, you'll need to hone your intuition, and the best way to do this is to have space dedicated to your spiritual and magical work. As a novice, you won't have to create an elaborate space - a simple altar will be more than enough to help you practice. Here is how to create a simple Wiccan altar.

Gathering Basic Supplies

First, you'll need a flat surface to work on. This can be anything from a simple tabletop to the top of your nightstand. Ensure you only keep items related to your intention or practice on it. Depending on your preferences, you can get a cloth to cover the altar as a means to define it as your sacred space. You'll need supplies to represent the four elements, the four directions, and the deity, spirit, or guide you're working with. Most Wiccan traditions recommend using a symbol for the god and the goddess. This can be as simple as using a bowl as a symbol of the divine feminine and a knife to represent masculine energy. Don't forget the pentagram, either. As an ultimate pagan symbol, the pentagram represents all four elements united in the first one - the spirit. Other supplies you need will be related to the specific work you plan to do and the season. Offerings and decorations like flowers, leaves, fruit, and veggies should all be seasonal.

Choosing the Location

Where you set up an altar depends on your preferences but also on your intention. Different purposes may require you to set up the altar in different directions. Here are some ideas on how to place your altar:

- **Facing East** - Is the most common choice as it corresponds to several intentions.

- **Facing South** - It works best for inspiration, courage, or making significant decisions.

- **Facing West** - This is the direction that symbolizes emotions and enhances them.

- **Facing North** - Associated with abundance and prosperity, the north is best when seeking growth.

Use a compass to identify the directions or follow the sun's movements. However, if you're working with limited space and have only one option, don't worry. You can always set up the altar where you can keep it long-term and enhance your intention in other ways.

Setting Up the Altar

Now it's time you place everything you gathered on your altar. Here is how to do it:

- Take a deep breath and release it slowly. Place the symbol of God and the Goddess in the center of the altar.

- Facing east, place the representation of the air element. In Wicca, this is typically done with feathers. These also represent the powers of the mind - both imaginative and rational. You're combining these two powers during your spiritual practice.

- Moving towards the south, you'll place the symbol of fire, like an orange candle (unlit) or a picture of a fire. It's associated with will, energy, power, and powerful animals. This applies only to the

Northern hemisphere. In the Southern hemisphere, fire is linked to the north.

- West can be represented by shells and other remnants of the creatures living in the water. It's linked to love and other fluid emotions.

- North is linked to the earth and is best represented by a cup of soil, salt, grains, or seeds. If you use the latter, you can take the seeds with you after your work is done and plant them somewhere where they can grow and thrive - or toss them out to feed the birds. Earth is also linked to life, so these are great ways to help nature create and nourish living beings.

- Spread any seasonal or intentional decorations (including the offerings) around the tools already on the altar.

- Place the pentagram in front of all the other tools and decorations.

- Take a deep breath and give thanks for what you were able to create. No matter how simple your altar is, the symbols you place on them will be as powerful as you make them.

- Invite the deities and spirits you want to work with and express gratitude for their help.

Making a Book of Shadows

The book of shadows is a collection of wisdom you gather over time. You'll need a blank notebook or maybe a binder. The latter is great for rearranging the contents later on. Whatever you choose, make sure it's good quality. After all, the book of shadows is a magical tool you'll use a lot - and it needs to last. Here are some ideas on what to include in your book:

- **Rules:** Even if you practice alone, you'll probably have boundaries and values you'll want to stick to. Write down what you think is acceptable to you and what's not.

- **Deities:** Whether you honor one deity, two, or more, it's a good idea to have a page dedicated to each of them. You can write any legends and correspondents associated with them, their preferred offerings, etc.

- **Dedication:** Recording the date you've become committed to a cause is a great way to honor it. You can dedicate yourself to a deity, spirit, healing, or other causes.

- **Correspondences:** Apart from the deities, you'll also need to learn the correspondences for the moon phases, energies, herbal ingredients, and much more. Enlisting them in your book of shadows will help you keep everything in one place so you can look up anything you need.

- **Significant Rituals and Ceremonies:** Record all the eight sabbats of the Wheel of the Year and the directions for any other rites and ceremonies you want to work on.

- **Recipes:** Your book of the shadow is also the perfect place to catalog all your recipes for healing concoctions, ointments, offerings, your unique recipes for holiday feasts, herbal blends, and much more.

- **Spells:** You can record the existing spells you prefer to work on or craft new ones - although many witches have a specific spellbook or grimoire for that purpose.

- **Divination:** If you practice divination, you can use your book of shadows to list all the information you need for your art. You can also record your sessions' results and revisit them to see how successful they were.

Casting a Circle

Wiccans use circles for protection, cleansing, and defining a place as sacred and safe for spells, rituals, and spiritual communication. A circle may also help you focus your energy - and the way you cast it will make everything even more personal. To form a sacred circle, you'll rely on the four directions and their associations with the four natural elements - just as you do when setting up an altar.

You'll Need the following:

- Salt - for the earth element

- Incense - for the fire element

- Feather - for the air element

- Water - for the water element

- A cloth to sit on (if you're working outside)

- A compass

- A space that's about 9ft in diameter
- A 4.5ft long cord
- A bundle of dried sage
- A crystal or a wand for directing the energy
- A symbol for the God and the Goddess

Instructions:

1. Gather all your supplies and find north on your compass. Lay out the cloth if you're outside.

2. Facing north, place the symbol of the male deity on your left side and the female one on your right side.

3. Take a few grounding breaths and visualize a green light enveloping your feet. Picture it traveling upwards toward your body.

4. Now visualize a white light enveloping your head and traveling down, meeting and mixing with the green one. When they do, they'll ground you and chase away the negative energy from and around you.

5. Visualize the lights departing and stretch your body to release any residual tension.

6. Take the string, and hold it over the salt while you place the latter on the north.

7. Turn the string slightly to the right to face east. Place the feather on the ground. You can secure it with a rock if you're outside.

8. Turn to face south and repeat with the incense, then finally with the water when facing West.

9. Facing one direction at a time, recite:

    "North, I welcome you, and I ask for your protection.

    East, I welcome you, and I ask for your wisdom.

    South, I welcome you, and I ask for your warmth.

    West, I welcome you, and I ask for your cleansing power."

10. Light the sage and start smudging your circle, starting North.

11. Walk in a clockwise direction 3 times while saying:

    "With the power of three, I banish negativity."

You can now cast the spell or perform the ritual of your choice. When you're done, don't forget to close the circle. The simplest way to do this is to face each direction and express your gratitude for their assistance in your work.

Simple Wiccan Spells and Rituals

Your best work will always be the one that's done with spells and rituals coming from your intention and tailored to fit it the best. However, if you're unsure where to begin, here are a few spells and rituals to help you get started on your Wiccan journey.

Freezing Spell against Bad Intentions

Whether it's people who spread rumors about you or someone who wants to harm you, these spells will help you against them. It's a harmless spell designed to keep toxic individuals away from you.

You'll Need the following:

- Water
- A zip-lock bag
- A piece of paper
- A pen or any other writing instrument

Instructions:

1. Fill up the bag with water. Leave about ⅓ at the top of the bag empty, so you can close it.
2. Write your intention on the paper. Be specific but leave room for a spell to work. For example, even if you want to keep a specific person out, don't use just their name. Write that you want the person to be bidden to stay away from you instead.
3. Fold the paper (so it fits the bag), and recite the following while focusing your energy on your intention:

   "I will now freeze this person out of my life to prevent them from hurting me."
4. Put the folded paper in the zip-lock bag with the water, and place it in the freezer.
5. Wait until the spell begins to work. Be patient, as this may take time, especially if you don't have too much experience yet.
6. When you feel the spell working, thaw the ice and bury the paper in the soil.

7. Pour the melted water over it and give thanks.

A Ritual for Success

This simple spell will help you manifest your wishes for success more efficiently. It works best for smaller goals, so remember to focus on the present when casting it.

You'll Need the following:

- Up to 20 drops of liquid camphor
- 1-2 large bay leaves
- A marker

Instructions:

1. Write your name and date of birth on one side of the bay leaves.
2. Write your intention on the other side of the leaves. Use short, present tense sentences, like:

   "I have a job."
3. While writing your intentions, focus on believing they've already come true.
4. Move the bay leaves in the air three times. This will communicate your wishes to the element.
5. Put the leaves in camphor, and let the letters dissolve slowly.
6. Take a final deep breath, and while you exhale, express gratitude to the air for granting you your wish.

Talisman with Protective Herbs

With this powerful talisman, you can protect yourself and your home from malicious influences. Activate it before significant magical work and when you think someone's trying to harm you with dark magic.

You'll Need the following:

- 1 Glass container with a lid
- 1 teaspoon of dried dill
- 1 teaspoon of dried and crushed bay leaves
- 1 teaspoon of dried sage
- 1 teaspoon of crushed black peppercorns

- 1 teaspoon of anise
- 1 teaspoon of garlic powder
- ½ cup of salt
- 1 teaspoon of fennel
- 1 teaspoon of dried basil
- 1 teaspoon of cloves

Instructions:

1. Place every ingredient in the jar, close it and shake it nine times to mix everything until well combined.
2. Then, recite the following spell:

   "Healing herbs and purifying salts of nine

   Help me guard this space of mine."
3. Place the jar on your altar if you only need protection for yourself and your sacred place during magical work.
4. If you need protection for your entire home, try setting the jar in the middle of your house. Make sure you keep it where it won't be disturbed. Moving it after setting it can reduce its effects.
5. Replace it every few months to ensure you remain protected from negative influences.

Disclaimers

Wiccan magic is highly personal. You rely on your own ability to manifest your desires. For this reason, you should only practice magic if you can keep your psychological and spiritual well-being in check. If your mental abilities are less than optimal for performing mundane tasks, you should not use them for magic, either. There are plenty of ways to boost your mental health, including meditation you can do at your altar. You can take advantage of the healing energy of the sacred space without focusing on the magic. Do a quick check of your mental state Before you start preparing for magical work and see if there are any stressors you have to deal with before you can proceed.

Wiccan traditions encourage using magic only for good and reject any negative purposes. Make sure that everything you do is for positive purposes and that you're allowed to do whatever you plan. Consult the deity or spiritual guide you plan to work with and ask them if it's a good idea.

Chapter 5: Norse Paganism and Asatru

Norse paganism is a set of beliefs and practices based on worshiping ancient Scandinavian gods. It is also known as Asatru, which means "faith in the gods." Norse paganism was the religion of the Viking people, who lived in what is now Scandinavia, Iceland, and Greenland. Today, many people practice Norse paganism, drawn to its rich mythology and practical worldview. Followers of the tradition believe in balancing these forces within themselves. They also believe that humans are an important part of the natural world and should live in harmony with nature.

Today, many people practice Norse paganism, drawn to its rich mythology and practical worldview.
https://www.pexels.com/photo/food-wood-nature-sun-6806402/

Norse paganism has a strong emphasis on personal growth and experimentation. Its practitioners believe that everyone has the potential to learn and grow, regardless of their background or station in life. As such, Norse pagans often seek out new experiences and perspectives. They value trials and challenges as opportunities to learn and grow. This open-minded approach to life can be refreshing for those who feel bogged down by the grind of everyday life.

In addition to its practical benefits, Norse paganism offers a deep connection to the natural world and our ancestors. For many people, this is a key reason for practicing this ancient faith. When we connect with nature, we remember that we are part of something larger than ourselves. We also remember our ancestors who came before us and the traditions they passed down. This can give us a sense of rootedness and belonging that is hard to find in today's fast-paced world.

This chapter will explore this fascinating religion's origins, history, and symbols. We will also examine the belief system and discuss some important concepts central to Norse paganism. Finally, we will look at some of the myths and legends associated with this faith.

Origins and History

The Norse pagan religion, also known as Asatru, is a polytheistic religion that stems from the practices of the ancient Germanic people. This ancient belief system is based on the pre-Christian mythology of northern Europe. Norse pagans believe in an afterlife and that the soul is reborn into another body after death. They also believe in reincarnation and that the world will one day be destroyed and rebuilt. Many modern pagans practice Asatru as a form of spirituality rather than religion. For them, it is a way to connect with their ancestors and nature. It is also a way to live in harmony with others and the world around them. Asatru is not just a set of beliefs but a way of life.

The ancient Norse people were polytheistic, meaning they worshiped multiple gods and goddesses. The most important deities in the Norse pantheon were Odin, Thor, and Freyja. These gods were associated with war, fertility, and wisdom, respectively. The Norse pantheon also included several other gods and goddesses, each of whom had their own areas of expertise. The Norse religion was based on a cosmology that revolved around the concept of nine worlds. Midgard, the world of humans, was considered the center of the universe by worshippers. There were four worlds surrounding Midgard: those of the giants, elves, dwarves, and the gods and goddesses. And in between these worlds, there was a mighty tree called Yggdrasil that linked them together. Norse Pagans believe in an afterlife and that those who die bravely in battle will spend eternity in Valhalla. They also believe in reincarnation and that souls can be reborn into different forms. Modern practitioners of Norse Paganism often hold rituals and celebrations outdoors, and many still live close to nature. For them, religion is not just a set of beliefs but a way of life.

Symbols and Cosmology

Norse paganism is a complex and fascinating belief system. It has a rich history and a truly unique cosmology. The most prominent symbol in Norse paganism is the hammer of Thor, which is a powerful symbol of protection. Other notable symbols include the Viking ship, which represents travel and exploration, and the Yggdrasil, which symbolizes the interconnectedness of all things. Valhalla is an integral part of Norse paganism as it is seen as a place where brave warriors can go after they die. It symbolizes the value of bravery and courage in Norse culture. Additionally, Valhalla provides comfort to those who lost loved ones in battle. They know that they are in a place where they can feast and fight forever.

Afterlife and Ancestor Worship in Norse Paganism

In Norse paganism, the concept of the afterlife and ancestor worship is deeply intertwined. For pagans, the afterlife is not a far-off, ethereal place where we go after death. Instead, it's a realm that exists alongside our own, separated only by a thin veil. Our ancestors live in this realm and can influence our lives—for good or bad. Ancestor worship is, therefore, a very important part of Norse paganism. It's believed that our ancestors can help us in times of need and that they have the power to intercede on our behalf with the gods. To honor our ancestors, modern practitioners often set up shrines in their homes where they keep pictures or other symbolic items that act as reminders. They also make offerings to them—food, drink, or other gifts—at these shrines. These offerings help nourish our ancestors' spirits and keep them happy, bringing blessings into our own lives. Ancestor worship is an important part of Norse paganism as it helps to connect the living with the dead. It is believed that ancestors can help guide and protect their descendants. Additionally, ancestor worship keeps the memory of loved ones alive. It is a way for people to connect with their past and remember those who have come before.

Belief System

The Norse people believed that when they died, their souls would go to either Valhalla (the hall of the slain) or Hel (the realm of the dead). Norse paganism teaches us that death is not the end. It is simply a transition into another stage of life. After we die, our souls go to the underworld, awaiting their final judgment. Suppose we have led good and honorable lives. In that case, we are rewarded with a place in Valhalla—the hall of the gods— where we feast and fight alongside Odin, Thor, and the other gods until the end of time. If we have not, however, our souls are sent to Hel—a dark and dismal realm ruled by the goddess Hela. The souls of murderers and other criminals are said to suffer horribly in Hel. It is, therefore, very important to live good lives so that we may enjoy happy afterlives with our ancestors in Valhalla.

Myths and Lore

The myths and legends associated with Norse paganism are some of the most fascinating stories in all of human history. The sagas and poems of the Norse people tell tales of gods and heroes, dragons and trolls. These stories are a window into the beliefs and values of the ancient Norse people and are often depicted in stories and artwork, which has led to several myths and lore linked to them.

Nordic mythology is full of fascinating and intriguing stories. Many of these stories involve powerful beings and heroic feats and are often steeped in mystery and magic. Some of the most well-known tales from Nordic mythology include the story of Ragnarok (the end of the world) and the story of Odin and his eight-legged horse, Sleipnir. These mythical beings often play an important role in the stories, and many of them have become iconic symbols of Nordic culture.

While some of the stories from Nordic mythology are dark and foreboding, others are lighthearted and fun. Many of the tales include elements of comedy, romance, and adventure. Regardless of their tone, all of the stories from Nordic mythology are fascinating and provide a glimpse into the culture and beliefs of the people who created them.

Heathenry

Heathenry is a polytheistic, indigenous European religion that emphasizes honor, courage, and familial bonds. Modern Heathenry has been influenced by various sources, including Norse mythology, the Icelandic sagas, and other Germanic traditions. Many Heathens see their religion as a way to connect with their ancestors and heritage. Heathenry is a reconstructionist religion, meaning its followers attempt to revive and recreate the beliefs and practices of the ancient Germanic peoples. This often includes studying the old myths and legends and trying to recreate our ancestors' lifestyles. While some people might see this as living in the past, Heathens believe that our ancestors were closer to nature and had a deeper understanding of the world around them.

While Heathenry is not an exclusive religion, most of its followers are of Germanic descent. This includes people from Scandinavia, the British Isles, Germany, Austria, and the Netherlands. In recent years, there has been a growing interest in Heathenry among people of other European backgrounds and those from North America and Australia. There are many different Heathen groups and organizations, each with its own unique take on the religion. Some focus on the worship of specific deities, while others emphasize community and fellowship. Heathens can be involved in various activities, from public rituals to private worship.

If you are interested in learning more about Heathenry, many resources are available online and in bookstores. There are also several active Heathen groups and organizations that can provide support and guidance. Whether you're looking to connect with your ancestry or learn more about ancient religion, Heathenry may be right for you.

Asatru

Even though the term Heathenry is used to refer to the entire religious movement.

Asatru is often preferred as a way to designate different groups within the religion. One of the main groups that followers belong to is Asatru.

The word "Asatru" comes from Old Norse and means "faith in the gods." In its modern form, Asatru is a reconstructionist religion that seeks to revive the polytheistic faith of the ancient Germanic peoples. Although there is no one "Asatru" tradition, common elements are found in many different Asatru practices. These include a focus on the worship of the

Aesir (the primary group of Germanic deities) and Vanir (a secondary group of deities), a belief in reincarnation, and the use of runes for divination. Asatru has its roots in the pre-Christian religion of the Germanic peoples. The first written record of Asatru dates back to the late 10th century when it was mentioned in the Icelandic Sagas. Since then, Asatru has undergone several changes and adaptations. In the early 21st century, there were an estimated 5,000-10,000 Asatruar (followers of Asatru) worldwide.

Asatruar believes in the existence of multiple gods and goddesses, each with its own areas of influence. Followers of this religion often celebrate the seasons and major events in the lives of the gods and goddesses. The most important holiday is Yule, which celebrates the sun's rebirth. Other holidays include Ostara (the spring equinox), Midsummer (the summer solstice), and Winternights (a festival honoring the dead).

Modern Asatru Practices

Asatruar typically practices their religion in small groups called "kindreds." These are often organized around a specific god or goddess. Many kindreds also participate in online forums and social media groups. There are several Asatru organizations, each with its own beliefs and practices. The largest Asatru organization is the Asatru Folk Assembly, founded in the United States in 1994. Other notable Asatru organizations include the Odinic Rite (founded in Britain in 1973) and the Ring of Troth (founded in the United States in 1987).

Asatru is an inclusive religion whose followers come from all walks of life. There are no strict rules or guidelines that Asatruar must follow, and people are free to believe and practice as they see fit. This flexibility has likely contributed to Asatru's popularity, as it allows people to tailor their beliefs and practices to their own needs and interests.

Although Asatru is a relatively new religion, it has significantly impacted the world. In recent years, Asatruar has been involved in several high-profile court cases, including one in which an Asatruar was granted the right to wear Thor's hammer pendant as part of his religious beliefs. Asatru is also making an impact beyond the courtroom. In Iceland, for example, an Asatru temple is currently being built, and it is thought to be the first of its kind in the world. This temple will serve as a gathering place for Asatruar and will be used for religious ceremonies and events.

The growth of Asatru is likely to continue in the years ahead as more people become interested in alternative religions. As Asatru becomes more mainstream, we will likely see a greater acceptance of this ancient belief system and its modern adaptations. Its popularity is likely due to several factors, including the rise of the internet and social media, which have made it easier for people to connect with others who share their beliefs. Additionally, the increased interest in paganism and alternative religions has also played a role in Asatru's growth.

Norse Rituals and Rites of Passage

Performing rituals was one way to please the gods and goddesses and to ask for their help or guidance. Different rituals could be performed for different purposes, such as giving thanks or offerings and asking for protection. One popular Norse ritual is called a Blot. This involves making an offering to the gods or goddesses, usually in the form of food or drink. The offering is then shared amongst those taking part in the ritual, and everyone says a prayer or gives thanks. Another popular Norse ritual is called a Sumbel. During this ritual, a horn of a bear or mead is passed around, and everyone drinks and toasts the gods and goddesses. Once again, prayers and thanks may be given during this ritual.

Norse rites of passage are also very meaningful. These can mark major life events such as birth, coming of age, marriage, and death. They often involve special ceremonies and rituals designed to help the person transition into their new phase of life. One of the most significant Norse rites of passage is called a Vala. This involves a woman giving birth in a special hut dedicated to the goddess Freyja. After the baby is born, it is washed in mead and then presented to the gods and goddesses. This ritual ensures that the child will be blessed by the gods and will have a long and prosperous life. Another significant rite of passage is their funeral ritual. In this process, the deceased's body is cremated, and their ashes are scattered at sea. This helps to ensure that their souls find their way to Valhalla, where they will feast and fight alongside the gods for eternity.

Norse rituals can be performed for various purposes, but they all serve to honor the gods and goddesses of Norse mythology. If you are interested in learning more about these rituals, you can take a Norse mythology class or attend a Viking festival.

Norse Magic

The ancient Norse people used runes for writing and divination. Rune is the Old Norse word for "secret" or "mystery." These magical symbols were used to preserve traditions and history and make predictions. Each rune had its own meaning and power, and the wise use of runes was said to be able to bring good fortune or ward off evil. There are different theories about the origins of runes, but most scholars believe that they were developed by the Germanic tribes who lived in northern Europe during the Iron Age. These tribes included the Angles, Saxons, and Jutes, who later migrated to Britain and gave their names to the countries of England, Scotland, and Wales. The runes began as a simplified form of writing, but they acquired magical properties over time. Runes were usually carved into pieces of wood or stone, although they could also be inscribed on metal, bone, or even cloth. The most famous Runes are the Elder Futhark, which consists of 24 symbols. The Elder Futhark was used throughout northern Europe during the Migration period and the early Middle Ages. The Younger Futhark, which has only 16 symbols, was used in Scandinavia during the Viking Age. Runes were also used for divination, and each symbol had its own meaning.

Norse Shamanism - Seidr

The practice of Norse shamanism, Seidr (which will be analyzed further in the following chapters), is an ancient tradition passed down through the generations. It is a form of magic used to connect with the spirits of nature and the cosmos. Seidr is a way of working with the energies of the universe to bring about change in one's life. It is also a way of accessing hidden knowledge and understanding the will of the gods. Seidr is traditionally practiced by those who are known as seers or shamans. These individuals can see into the future and receive guidance from the spirits. Seers can also enter into trances, allowing them to contact the spirits directly. Shamans can use their abilities to help others in their community.

Seidr is a very personal practice, and each shaman has unique ways of working with the spirits. Some use drums or other musical instruments to help them enter into a trance state. Others use chanting or singing to reach the spirit world. The practice of Seidr is not just about entering into trances or contacting spirits. It is also about working with the universe's energies to bring about change. Seers use their abilities to influence the course of events. They can heal the sick, find lost objects, and even bring rain to dry land. Seidr is a powerful tool that can be used for both good and evil.

Seidr is a mystery, and there is much we do not understand about it. However, those practicing it know it is a real and powerful force. Seidr is an important part of Norse culture, and its traditions continue to this day.

The Old Norse religion is an intricate and fascinating belief system that has been around for centuries. It contains interesting stories, myths, and lore that teach us about our ancestors and their beliefs. While there are many aspects of this tradition that we may not be able to understand or agree with today, these beliefs held great importance to the people who practiced them. The Norse religion and its traditions can provide us with a wealth of knowledge about ourselves and life itself. A great deal of meaning is found today in this religion's rituals and mythology, which are important to many people.

Chapter 6: Walking the Seiðr Path

Seidr was the Norse world's most common form of magic and was mainly concerned with issues of fate. Its practitioners could see the traces of fate and subtly change them however they wanted. Their knowledge of divination was used for both good and evil purposes. While they were able to cast curses that hurt people, they also performed protective spells and charms to help others and keep them safe. Those who performed this type of magic typically led nomadic lifestyles, which is why they were not trusted among community members.

The Norse god Odin on his horse Sleipnir.
https://commons.wikimedia.org/wiki/File:Ardre_Odin_Sleipnir.jpg

While women who practiced Seidr were highly respected, men who did it were often scorned. Seidr had an aura of secrecy associated with it, which was a feminine trait in Norse traditions and culture. This is why men who practiced Seidr were thought to be breaking gender norms. This way of thinking also applies to the deities. Even though Odin was believed to be the most skillful practitioner of Seidr in existence, he was mocked for using feminine powers despite his other masculine characteristics.

In this chapter, we'll explore what Seidr is. You'll learn what a Völva is and understand the different levels of trance a shaman can reach. Then, you'll come across a step-by-step guide on how to cast a protective circle, induce a trance state, and practice grounding visualization.

What Is Seidr?

Seidr is a form of Norse shamanism and magic that predates Christianity. It was mainly practiced foretelling fate, identify its path, and manipulate its inner workings to create change. Practitioners could do that by using symbolism to weave desired situations and events into reality. They performed rituals to transport themselves into a trance where they could communicate with the spirit world. Their tasks were mostly done to perform a curse, a blessing, or a prophecy.

Seidr rituals weren't limited to divination and matters of fate. They were also used for clairvoyance, allowing the practitioner to discover the locations of hidden objects and the secrets of the mind. Seidr was also used to heal the sick, attract abundance and good luck, call in fish and animals for food, and control the weather. When used for malicious purposes, Seidr was used to cast curses, such as inducing sickness or making any land barren. Some shamans also told people false futures to lead them toward the wrong, often disastrous, path. Some recipients injured and killed their adversaries in domestic disagreements and during periods of battle due to false readings. Those who mastered the art of weaving to manipulate or change fate were known as the Norns. They were considered to be the most proficient practitioners.

The god Odin and the goddess Freya are two significant Vanir and Aesir deities who mastered the art of Seidr. They were divine archetypes of male and female practitioners. Since this form of magic was very gendered, particularly during the Viking age, it's necessary to keep this distinction in mind.

What Is a Völva?

The goddess Freya modeled the role of the völva. A völva was a woman practitioner of Seidr during the Viking age. Freya is the first deity to bring this type of magic to the realm of the gods. A Völva had an esteemed role in the community as she was considered a healer or spiritual leader in her society. She was usually close to her clan's leaders. Male seidr practitioners were called seers and were rare to find.

A Völva never settled in one area but traveled around different cities. She was offered accommodation in return for magical practices. You can learn more about the Völva from ancient sagas and other transcripts.

Even though they were treated respectfully, Völvas were somewhat segregated from society in negative and positive nuances. A Völva was feared and often stigmatized yet sought-after and esteemed. She is highly comparable to the Veleda, a Germanic prophetess who was very respected among her tribe.

According to Viking culture and traditions, Seidr was considered an inappropriate activity for men. People then were expected to comply with stringent gender roles, which is why it was considered taboo for men to partake in any women-like practices. Therefore, men who practiced Sedr were thought to be "unmanly." This label was a substantial insult to Viking men.

There were numerous reasons for the shunning of male practitioners. Perhaps the most notable is the weaving aspect of the practice, which was among the primary economic contributions of Viking women. That said, some men still engaged in Seidr and even regarded it as their occupation. A few of them had their works recorded in historical sagas.

The leading seer was, of course, the god Odin. Despite his greatness, he was still called unmanly by some. This disapproval, however, often came with nuances of hesitation and uncertainty. Even though practicing this form of magic was perceived as feminine, whoever could do it held immense power. Some male practitioners thought that the perception of society was a small price to pay for the abilities that Seidr offered. Besides, they had none other than Odin, the mighty king of Asgard, to look up to.

Different Levels of Trance

For millennia, humans all across the globe have used numerous techniques to enter trance states, or "altered states of consciousness." Shamans and indigenous groups across nations believed that this state acted as a bridge between the unconscious mind and the world of spirit.

Very few people realize that most major universal belief systems, such as Hinduism and the 3 Abrahamic religions, also have practices that incite subtle trance states. This allows practitioners to connect more effectively with the divine, which essentially grows their faith.

Regardless of your spiritual beliefs, entering a trance state offers numerous benefits, especially if you intend to practice any form of magic.

How Does a Trance State Feel Like?

A trance state is a frame of mind you enter when you're neither sleeping nor entirely conscious. Being in an altered state of consciousness requires you to transport between the conscious and subconscious mind. It's somewhat like zoning out" of reality.

The 5 Levels of Trance State

There are five levels of an altered state of consciousness:

Level 1: Very Light Trance

The first level requires you to increase your self-awareness of your thoughts, feelings, and physical sensations. This state of mind can be accessed via mindful meditation.

Level 2: Light Trance

This frame of mind resembles what it's like to be dreaming. We all experience this altered state of consciousness without realizing it. We all often zone out while driving or reading and just do it automatically.

Level 3: Medium Trance

This trance state entirely shifts your consciousness from your environment. You lose the sense of time and control, or even awareness, of your body.

Level 4: Deep Trance

This is the level of consciousness you'd access if you were hypnotized. The latter is the rapid and somewhat confusing state of consciousness that happens right before you drift off and your conscious mind goes to bed. People who fall into a deep trance usually hallucinate.

Level 5: Very Deep Trance

At this stage, you completely lose consciousness. It is similar to being in a coma or experiencing very deep, dreamless sleep.

Levels 2, 3, and 4 are ideal for spiritual practices.

Step-By-Step Guide

Before we delve into various techniques and exercises, you must know that you should conduct shamanic practices under the supervision of a professional guide. If you wish to practice alone, you must grow your knowledge and expertise in trance and journeying techniques before you move further ahead. It goes without saying that anyone struggling with mental health should not engage in shamanic practices or other rituals.

Casting a Protective Circle

Casting a magic circle can help cleanse and purify your space from undesirable energies. It can help you handle negative people in your life, protect your space from soaking up bad energy, and maintain your peace even if someone is trying to bring you down. People who notice a strange presence or energy in their houses, such as sudden waves of cold air, bizarre noises, and recurrent nightmares, can cast a protective circle to eliminate the unwanted presence.

Magic circles don't only help you get rid of malicious spirits, but they also attract good ones to enter your space. This practice also allows you to direct your own powers toward a sole purpose, which is providing protection and safety from all kinds of harm. You should not attempt any magic ceremony without the presence of a magic circle because otherwise, you wouldn't be able to keep your spell safe from any external, interfering forces. Magic circles help you focus on your intent.

There are numerous ways to cast a magic circle. While some are very simple, others can get extremely complicated. The most popular ways, however, are "Calling in the Four Directions" and "Lesser Banishing Ritual of the Pentagram." The former pertains to indigenous shamanism and is the simpler option. The former comes from Western magical tradition.

Whichever ritual you choose to perform, you need to face each of the four directions so you can pay homage to their power. The shamans embody the directions as animal totems, while in the second method, they are embodied as the Four Archangels. You need to provide an offering of burning tobacco or sage to call in the Four Directions. Some people prefer to raise their hands with their palms facing outward instead.

Face each of the directions as you say the following prayer:

"Guardian of the South, totem of the Serpent, power of the Heart, grant us the gift of your Water medicine so that we may give with our emotions freely and honestly, loving unconditionally.

Guardian of the West, totem of the Jaguar, power of the Body, grant us the gift of your Earth medicine so that we may hold with our bodies, enduring our challenges with strength and grace.

Guardian of the North, totem of the Hummingbird, power of the Mind, grant us the gift of your Air medicine so that we may receive with our minds, always open to wisdom and insight.

Guardian of the East, totem of the Eagle, power of the Spirit, grant us the gift of your Fire medicine, so that we may determine with our spirits, living our lives in harmony with the Great Spirit."

Then, return to your initial position and place your hand over your heart as you recite the rest of the prayer:

"In honor of our ancestors, the star people, the stone people, the plant people, our animal brothers and sisters, sages, healers and teachers past, present and future, and all who dwell herein.

In honor of Mother Earth below, who sustains us. In honor of Father Sky above, who guides us. In honor of the Great Spirit throughout, who has ten thousand names and is the unnamable one.

A-ho!"

Since this is a protection spell, you can tweak the prayer to vocalize your wishes and concerns to your guardians more directly. You can ask them to protect you from the forces that wish to harm you or eliminate any unwanted energies from your life. Suppose you believe you've been subject to a magical attack, which is a very rare occurrence. In that case, you can cast the circle and remain inside it for the entire duration of this attempt. You can absorb sufficient protective power if you sleep inside the circle until sunrise.

Once you've completed your ceremony, you need to close the magic circle by repeating the prayer we mentioned above. However, instead of asking the guardians for their protection or medicine, you should thank them for granting it to you instead. Say your goodbyes before exiting the circle.

Inducing a Trance State

There are a plethora of methods you can try out to induce a trance state. However, the following are among the most popular and easiest techniques to experiment with:

Breathwork:

Changing the rhythm and pace of your breathing is among the most common methods to bring oneself into a trance state. If you're already familiar with some breathing practices, such as pranayama, you can use them to transport yourself into an altered state of consciousness. It doesn't matter which technique you use as long as it's comfortable and doesn't feel forced. You can facilitate the process of entering a trance level of awareness by practicing pranayama or other breathing exercises. This is because these practices allow you to release all mental blocks that hold you back.

Another very popular technique is known as Holotropic breathwork. This practice involves the maintenance of quick and regulated breathing patterns. You must consult your doctor before trying any breathing exercises if you struggle with any health problems.

Recite Mantras and Prayers:

Repeating certain words, making repetitive sounds, or reciting mantras can also be quite helpful. Monks of various religions, including Hinduism, Christianity, and Buddhism, suggest that reciting a mantra can help you alter your consciousness. Prayers mostly only lead to a light state of trance. However, working with prayers that call to you and experimenting with using them in different and unconventional ways can help you transcend the limits of the conscious brain.

Primal Sounds, Beats, and Rhythms:

Have you ever wondered why drums are among the first few elements that come to mind when people think of shamans? Drums are a great way to trigger the trance state that a person needs to embark on their inner journeying practice.

While you can get a bongo, hand drum, or any other drum you like, listening to a primal rhythmic playlist on YouTube will do the trick. Listening to throat singing from indigenous cultures, binaural beats, or repetitive music can be helpful. Avoid listening to songs with words in them unless they're repetitive and are in a language you can't understand. You want to keep your conscious mind as uninvolved as possible.

Grounding Visualization

Step 1: Start by standing with your feet spread apart. Position them firmly on the ground and keep them aligned with your shoulders. Put your arms above your head and extend your fingers toward the ceiling.

Step 2: Visualize bursts of energy leaving the end of your spine and down the soles of your feet. Like tree roots, visualize all this energy digging deep into the ground, penetrating the foundation of your home, the pavement, or the grass. Keep envisioning these roots as they dig through the Earth's soil and crust. Imagine this energy as it travels through the magma and to the planet's core. Feel the energy you can draw from it as it wraps itself around it.

Step 3: Visualize branches growing from your spine, passing through your neck, and reaching out to your head. Visualize branches growing through your arms and through the palms of your hands. Imagine how they would look as they grow higher and into the sky. Envision them as they penetrate the stratosphere reaching through the center of the Universe until they reach the source of creation. Again, imagine the branches as they tap and surround the source, drawing down this energy to you.

Step 4: Imagine yourself as you fill up with all the energy coming from above and below you together. Visualize the divine universal and earthly energies as they combine inside you, making you whole. Visualize this scenario for as long as you need to.

Step 5: Whenever you're ready, visualize the branches as they come back inside. Feel them as they recede into you. Envision the roots receding from the Earth and into your being.

Step 6: Take a couple of deep breaths and bring yourself back to reality.

Now that you have read this chapter, you know everything that you need to know about seidr and its practitioners. You also understand the importance of reaching an altered state of consciousness when practicing inner journeying. Light to deep trance states is ultimately the most effective to work with. Doing breathwork, reciting prayers and mantras, and listening to primal sounds, beats, and rhythms are some of the simplest and most common methods that you can use to induce an altered state of consciousness.

Chapter 7: Runes: History and Theory

Now that you've learned a little more about Norse mythology, you are ready to delve into the use of the runes. These ancient symbols had several purposes throughout history - and this chapter will uncover all of them. You'll see how their use evolved from a complex communication instrument to a simple divination tool, as it is widely known today.

The History of Runes

The early records and the Norse tales indicate that the runes were primarily a communication tool developed by Germanic tribes and used as far back as 50 C.E. However, the earliest known evidence of the runes used as a writing form is documented in a carving that dates back to 400 C.E. According to the lore, the runes were revealed to people by Odin himself. He discovered them during the ordeal he suffered when he was forced to spend nine days and nights hanging from Yggdrasil, also called the "Tree of Life." After the ninth night, he looked down, saw the runes, and was suddenly able to free himself. Although he wielded great power over his followers, Odin realized that the runes held even more wisdom than he possessed and decided to share them with the rest of the deities. He taught them their meaning and use, and, in turn, they passed on this knowledge to people.

People then began to use the runes as letters, organizing them into an alphabet. However, for the ancient Norse, the meaning of each letter wasn't as simple as it is in modern languages. According to them, each rune symbolizes a specific form of energy, a universal thought, or simply an aspect of life. Because of this complex relationship between the runes and their symbolism, the runes were used only by the most educated tribe members. They used the runes to record events and prophecies affecting the tribe or to communicate with other tribes, exchanging information and forging alliances. The primary meaning of the term rune was "mystery" or "message that needs to be kept secret."

The Norse also believed that runes could unlock the future and enable communication across different worlds. According to several Norse myths, runes had magical properties. These allowed people to send and receive messages from higher beings, inducing the deities, ancestral spirits, animals, and even magical inanimate objects.

Each rune was named after what it represented - both in a magical sense and the philosophical one. The runes were initially carved into stone templates, which stood as a testimony to the tribe's hierarchy and achievements. Later, people began to inscribe them on small pieces of stone, bone, metal, or wood and carry them around so they could use them for different purposes. Nowadays, you'll find runes carved or painted on talismans, used as body ink, or written on a piece of paper during magical practices. How runes are written is linked to how their name sounds and which letter they represent in the Norse alphabet. For example, the Tiwaz rune is pictured as an upward-pointed arrow. This depicts the rune as the symbol of the god of war and his habit of traveling across the sky.

Runic alphabets are named "Futharks," after the runes Fehu, Uruz, Thurisaz, Ansuz, Raidho, and Kenaz. These were the first six runes of the oldest known runic alphabet, the Elder Futhark. This alphabet contains 24 runes, which are equivalent to a large number of letters in the Old English language. Most evidence of the use of the Elder Futhark runes has been found on coins, weapons, and garments dating from the Iron Age. In fact, Elder Futhark is still used today, although only for divination and not for writing or communication. The runes in this alphabet were divided into three aetts - each ruled over by a powerful Norse deity. Each aett also represents a specific stage in life - from the earliest success to failure to prospering despite the difficulties.

While the first full alphabet letters were harsh and complex characters, the more recent version, the Younger Futhark, was simpler and contained only 16 runes. This was introduced around 750 CE, with the arrival of the Viking Age. It eventually replaced its predecessor as a writing form throughout Scandinavia. According to historical evidence, at this time, the new runes were used in markets and artifacts depicting the heroic achievements of the tribes. The characters of the Younger Futhark were faster to write, which presumably saved the Vikings time for writing them, so they could be focused on battling instead. Another version, the Anglo-Saxon Futhorc, was developed in England. This one was the expansion of the Elder Futhark - from 24 to 33 characters.

Germanic traditions were often centered around fate, as this determined whether they would survive or fall victim to their enemy or the harsh environment they were surrounded by. Countless tales depict how the runes revealed fate or helped people alter it when needed. One of the tales showing how the runes helped alter a person's fate is also tied to their privilege as a writing tool. It comes from a period where only some people were skilled at rune carving, but many tried their chances with them. It begins with the great Viking Egil traveling across a farmer's land and learning that the farmer's child is very ill. In exchange for a meal, Egil offered to see if he could help the child. Upon entering the child's room, Egil noticed a piece of whalebone with rune carvings near the child's bed. Since he was versed in runic inscriptions, Egil learned that the runes on the whalebones (inscribed by someone who barely knew the runes) carried a negative message. He was sure that this caused the child to become ill. Egil replaced the whalebone with a piece of stone which contained a positive message, encouraging the child to recover - which they did.

Tales like the one above suggest a clear distinction between the different uses for the runes. Some runes were only meant to be used for communication, while others could be used for magical and other purposes. Despite this, some didn't respect this rule. Whether due to ignorance or malice, some still used the runes for inappropriate purposes. Followers of the ancient Norse traditions in modern times still claim that the different uses of the runes must be considered at all times. Beginners are advised to learn the meaning and association of each rule before attempting to use it - even for writing their names or simple messages.

The Meaning of Runes

The runes of the Elder Futhark have several meanings, and they're often open to the reader's interpretation. That said, here are the aspects of life each rune is associated with, along with their symbols and English equivalents. Their uses in magical practices will be discussed further on. However, you can also use them to translate short texts from English to Norse. For example, you can write your name or simple sentences. Keep in mind that the letters are not duplicated in the futhark. If you have the same letter twice in your name or the text you're trying to translate, you should only write the corresponding rune once.

Freyr's Aett

As the fertility god, Freyr is often associated with creativity, productivity, and the beginning of a new life. The runes in his aett reflect one's ability to create and find their place on the material plane.

ᚠ - Fehu

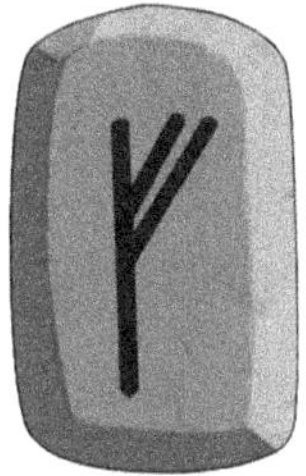

Fehu Rune.
https://pixabay.com/es/illustrations/fehu-runa-fe-runa-adivinaci%c3%b3n-6508602/

English equivalent: F

Pronounced "FAY-hoo," the name of this rune literally means cattle. However, in broad terms, it can also be translated to abundance, wealth, hope, property, luck, fortune, and material gain. It's also said to symbolize the fulfillment of foals and dreams in all aspects of life.

ᚢ- Uruz

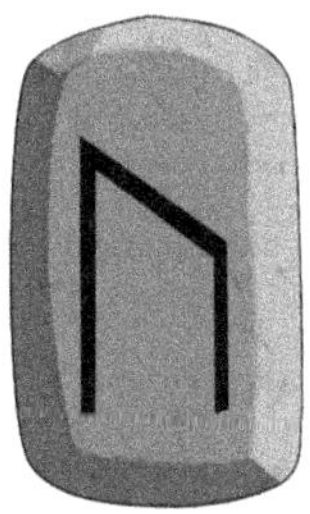

Uruz Rune.
https://pixabay.com/es/illustrations/uruz-ur-runa-futhark-n%c3%b3rdico-6508604/

English equivalent: U

Pronounced "OO-rooz," Uruz in English means "wild ox." Like this magnificent animal, the rune is linked to the strength of will, courage, endurance, vitality, health, perseverance, and good times in general. It is believed that Uruz has the power to shape one's destiny through challenges.

Þ - Thurisaz

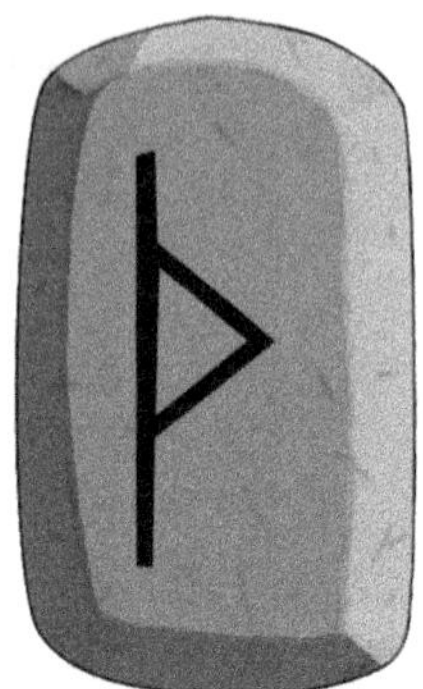

Thurisaz Rune.
https://pixabay.com/es/illustrations/thurisaz-jueves-runa-futhark-6508603/

English equivalent: Th

Pronounced "THUR-ee-sazh," this rune is translated as "giant" in English. It can also symbolize the hammer of Thor, protection, defense, disruptive forces, attack, or danger. Thurisaz means that you must change course and adopt a new one to harness divine power.

ᚠ - Ansuz

Ansuz Rune.
https://pixabay.com/es/illustrations/ansuz-runa-runas-futhark-2644294/

English equivalent: A

Pronounced "AHN-sooz," this rune means revelation. It is linked to Odin and his ability to communicate. It can also point toward other Norse deities who may send messages and insight through visions and signs. It's also said to illustrate mental capacity, the mouth, and organs needed for speech.

ᚱ - Raidho

Raidho Rune.
https://pixabay.com/es/illustrations/raidho-runa-runas-futhark-2644605/

English equivalent: R

Pronounced "Rah-EED-ho," this rune is translated as a "journey on horseback." It can also signify any form of movement, progress in life, spiritual growth, the discovery of new perspectives, or the conscious decision to work for your goals and channel your energy for better results.

ᚲ - Kenaz

Kenaz Rune.
https://pixabay.com/es/illustrations/kenaz-runa-runas-futhark-2644856/

English equivalent: C / K

Pronounced "KEN-ahz," Kenaz is a Norse term for ulcer. It may also mean torch, transformation, passion, enlightenment, insight, or a purpose. Some believe the rune is the sight of receiving a higher calling towards following one's dreams. It's a sign that outside influences need to remain where they are.

X - Gebo

Gebo Rune.

https://pixabay.com/es/illustrations/gebo-runa-runas-futhark-2644831/

English equivalent: G

Pronounced "GHEB-o," this tune means "gift" in English. It's often referred to as a sign of gratitude or the need to exchange something through offerings. Gebo represents the way to obtain assistance, partnership, service, or luck through acts of generosity, charity, and providing what you expect in return.

ᚹ - Wunjo

Wunjo Rune.

https://pixabay.com/es/illustrations/wunjo-runa-runas-futhark-2644556/

English equivalent: W

Pronounced "WOON-yo," this rune represents joy and happiness. It may also mean the fulfillment of dreams and general well-being that may be threatened by an impending change. Wunjo brings destruction and tests one's strengths to see if one can maintain the ability to grow and thrive.

Heimdall's Aett

As the gatekeeper of the ancient gods, Heimdall ensures that only the ones able to show maturity and growth will prosper. His aett contains runes that lead to happiness through a journey of expansion and success.

ᚺ - Hagalaz

Hagalaz Rune.
https://pixabay.com/es/illustrations/hagalaz-runa-runas-futhark-2644694/

English equivalent: H

Pronounced "HA-ga-lah," this rune means "hail" in English. It represents difficulties that may halt plans or delay them at least. It may also refer to external input or the wrath of nature, which often has uncontrollable effects. It is said that Hagalaz can change one's life for the better.

ᚾ - Naudhiz

Naudhiz Rune.
https://commons.wikimedia.org/wiki/File:Runic_letter_naudiz.svg

English equivalent: N

Pronounced "NOWD-heez," Naudhiz is translated as "need." It can also mean resistance, distress, lacking, or difficulty thriving. However, in most cases, it symbolizes the necessity to overcome a challenge and manifest one's wishes and the ways to stop ignoring one's issues and unfulfilled desires.

| - Isa

Isa Rune.

English equivalent: I

Pronounced "EE-sa," this rune means "ice." It signals a sudden period of stillness when the world or a specific action must stop so you can see the changes you need to make. It's believed that Isa is needed for successful renewal. Otherwise, you'll keep following the same old patterns and remain stuck.

⛋ - Jera

Jera Rune.

English equivalent: J / Y

Pronounced "YARE-a," Jera sounds very similar to its English translation - year. The appearance of this rune means harvest, rewards for hard work, life cycle, and conclusion of a period. At the same time, it also symbolizes new beginnings, opportunities for growth, and gathering abundance and wisdom.

ʃ - Eihwaz

Eihwaz Rune.
https://pixabay.com/es/illustrations/eihwaz-runa-runas-futhark-2644633/

English equivalent: E / I

Pronounced "AY-wahz," this rune means "yew." As the symbol of ultimate wisdom, the yew tree represents uncovering the mysteries of life, finding inspiration, stability, the connection to the sacred wisdom and the divine. Eihwaz may also show you how to overcome a challenge through sacrifice.

ᛈ - Perthro

Perthro Rune.
https://pixabay.com/es/illustrations/perthro-runa-runas-futhark-2644941/

English equivalent: P

Pronounced "PER-thro," Perthro represents fate, prophecy, the occult, and mysticism. It may also mean fertility, self-awareness, and the chance to discover new ways to improve your fortune. When this rune appears, you can be sure that your future depends on your current choices.

ᛉ - Algiz

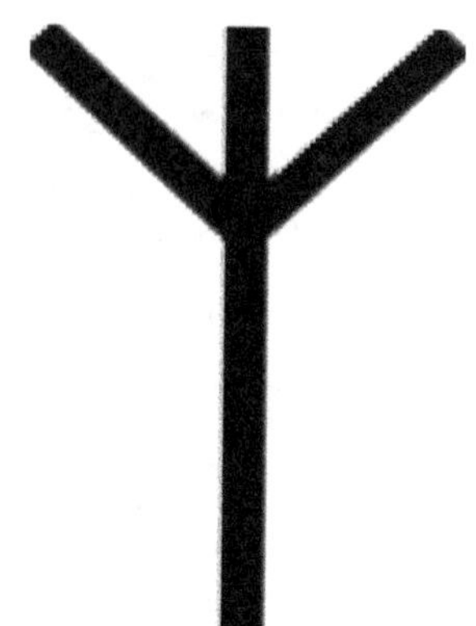

Algiz Rune.
https://commons.wikimedia.org/wiki/File:Runic_letter_algiz.svg

English equivalent: Z

Pronounced "AL-geez," this rune means "elk." This animal is associated with good luck, courage, protection, and awakening. It signals that you must rely on your gut feelings to find the connection to your higher spiritual self. Algiz shows that your instincts are there to protect you.

ᛋ - Sowilo

Sowilo Rune.
https://pixabay.com/es/illustrations/sowilo-runa-runas-futhark-2644331/

English equivalent: S

Pronounced "So-WEE-lo," Sowilo means "sun" in English. This celestial body symbolizes solace, vitality, abundance, motivation, joy, and much more. Whatever challenge you may face, this rune provides reassurance that you'll persevere against them.

Tyr's Aett

Tyr, the powerful god of the skies, is the ultimate Norse symbol of war and justice. The runes in his aett refer to spiritual development and one's ability to create a legacy one can be proud of.

↑ - Tiwaz

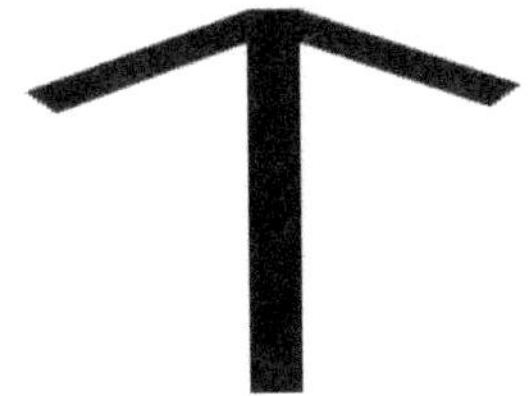

Tiwaz Rune.
https://commons.wikimedia.org/wiki/File:Runic_letter_tiwaz.png

English equivalent: T

Pronounced "TEE-wahz," this rune is translated as "the god Thor." It represents this deity's attributes, including bravery, leadership, honor, and strength. It can also mean making sacrifices for the greater good and thriving despite all challenges and difficulties.

ß - Berkano

Berkano Rune.
https://pixabay.com/es/illustrations/berkana-runa-runas-futhark-2644529/

English equivalent: B

Pronounced "BER-Kah-no," Berkano means "birch," also linked to the birch goddess. It is associated with fertility, rebirth, and the beginning of a new project or relationship. The rune can also signal the potential for growth and find creative ways to begin anew or obtain sustenance.

ᛗ - Ehwaz

Ehwaz Rune.
https://pixabay.com/es/illustrations/ehwaz-runa-runas-futhark-2644896/

English equivalent: E

Pronounced "EH-wahz," this rune means "horse." In Norse mythology, this animal is the symbol of trust. Besides this, the rune may convey partnership, companionship, and faith in one's progress. It can also signify animal instinct, the need for assistance, or moving forward with your life.

ᛗ - Mannaz

Mannaz Rune
https://pixabay.com/es/illustrations/mannaz-runa-runas-futhark-2644241/

English equivalent: M

Pronounced "MAN-Naz," Mannaz is the rune for the English word "man." This means it represents humanity, mortality, and the balance between life and death. It's also believed to symbolize community and human traits like values and skills one develops throughout life.

ᛚ - Laguz

Laguz Rune.

https://pixabay.com/es/illustrations/laguz-runa-runas-futhark-2644773/

English equivalent: L

Pronounced "LAH-gooz," this rune has several meanings. Commonly linked to water and fluidity, potential, inner awareness, and the unknown. It also represents imagination, dreams, and ways to heal emotions by remaining open even through difficult times.

◇ - Ingwaz

Ingwaz Rune.

https://commons.wikimedia.org/wiki/File:Runic_letter_ingwaz.png

English equivalent: Ng

Pronounced "ING-wahz," the name of this rune is linked to the god of Ingwaz. Its meaning varies from new beginnings to finding your potential through new energies, sexuality, family, ancestral wisdom, and more. It also represents peace and natural spiritual growth.

ᛟ - Othala

Othala Rune.

https://pixabay.com/es/illustrations/othala-runa-runas-futhark-2644445/

English equivalent: O

Pronounced "OH-tha-la," this rune means "inheritance." It's also linked to traditions, heritage, homecoming, inherent talents, nobility, ancestral wisdom, and property. It may also indicate that your values lie in your legacy and connection to Othala and your community.

ᛞ - Dagaz

Dagaz Rune.

https://pixabay.com/es/illustrations/dagaz-runa-runas-futhark-2644493/

English equivalent: D

Pronounced "DAH-gahz," Dagaz is a Norse term for "day." It means hope, inspiration, the possibility of awakening, balance, significant changes at the beginning of the day, and the beginning of a new cycle. It can also signify happiness, clarity, spiritual growth, and self-consciousness.

Chapter 8: Working with Runes

As you've learned from the previous chapter, divination is one of the most prevalent uses of Norse runes. By the end of this chapter, you'll learn more about divinatory practices using the runic alphabet. You'll also receive several tips and formats for casting your own runic layouts and learning how to find answers to your own future-related questions.

Runes can be cast in several ways, either randomly or in a specific pattern.
https://www.pexels.com/photo/runic-letters-on-wood-chunks-and-ground-with-autumn-leaves-10110445/

Runic Divination

Looking into future outcomes with runes or rune casting is one of the easiest divinatory methods. Similarly to Tarot readings, the runes are laid or tossed on a flat surface and then interpreted. The runes can be cast in several ways, either randomly or in a specific pattern - with each rune having a specific purpose. Runic divination is used for answering simple questions to help you make a decision regarding your future. It's not fortune-telling, and it won't give you specific answers. The runes may reveal different influences related to your questions and answers. However, they'll never tell you a specific time of the day when something will happen. The runes represent the gateway to your subconscious - and by presenting their symbols in front of you, they'll guide you to find the answers that are already in your subconscious.

In ancient times, the runes were symbols carved on small sticks made from branches of nut-bearing trees. Traditionally, the runes were cast randomly on a piece of white cloth. The runecaster said a quick prayer to the gods or spirits they asked to help interpret the results and looked up to the sky while tossing the runes in front of them. They would then interpret the results according to their practices. Nowadays, you can buy runes in the form of small stones, rocks, bone, metal, or wooden objects with symbols carved or painted on them. Stones are typically the best options, as they are more durable, and there are fewer chances of rubbing the symbols off during use. You can even make these yourself, allowing you to form a stronger personal connection and charge them with your energy much more efficiently. That said, crafting your runes is a magical process that takes practice and knowledge. You may want to rehearse with some ready-made versions before committing to making your own. You can also buy crystal runes. These already come with powerful magic of their own, but you can infuse them with even more.

Casting the Runes

You can follow the ancient technique of tossing out the runes on a piece of white fabric or use some of the modern methods, such as laying them out on your altar (or a flat surface in your sacred space if you don't have an altar). It's recommended to face west while casting the runes, but if your practice requires you to face any other direction, you can do it that way. The method you opt for is a highly personal choice. Feel free to try whatever feels right. Keep your runes in a safe space, preferably in a pouch or box - which helps protect them from negative influences. Before you delve into any layouts, always cleanse your space, yourself, and your runes to ensure nothing will limit your ability to correctly interpret the answers.

Once you've dispelled any negative energy and prepared your mind and body for the reading, you can begin the casting. Put your hands into the container and mix your runes. Then, remove a number while formulating the appropriate question. It helps newbies consider the question even before you take out the runes. If needed, meditate on what you're interested in for 5-10 minutes before casting. Make sure you ask simple but specific questions. Try tossing one rune first and observing it as it lands. Has it landed face up or face down? Runes landing face up are the answer to the questions. Later, you can try casting three runes - these will also reveal the past and future influences related to your question. Traditionally, the runes were cast in odd numbers, and most modern layouts carried this approach.

Interpreting the Results

Since each rune has a different meaning, the results will always depend on how you interpret them. For example, Ansuz means "message." However, it can also mean inspiration, advice, or even enthusiasm. It's up to you to discern what this rune means to you under specific circumstances. You may improve your communication, seek advice on an important matter, or a new truth will be revealed to you in the future. You'll need to tap into your intuition to understand which answer is correct. While doing so, consider any future events, situations, or circumstances that Ansuz could apply. When could it come in handy? How could it help grow and prosper? Don't second guess whatever you see the answer to be. The first thing that comes to mind is typically the closest one to the answer you're looking for. If your gut tells you to seek advice on something, it is probably right.

Runes only provide hints and not exact answers. You'll need to hone your intuition and critical thinking abilities to learn how to interpret them correctly. You should also keep in mind that the future isn't fixed. When you change a single aspect that influences your future, the outcome will turn out differently from what you've predicted. This will happen no matter how precisely you've interpreted the answers in the present time. Anytime you change your thoughts and behavior, you're also changing your future. Practicing with the runes can be a great way to develop intuition. Besides teaching you how to shape your future to your liking, runic divination also promotes spiritual growth and happiness.

If you're tossing the runes, the interpretation also depends on the way they land. If you are just starting, you can choose to interpret only the ones that landed upright, as these provide more direct answers. Once you get the hang of it, you can try reading the ones that landed face down. These showcase hidden issues and truths. Like Tarot cards, Norse runes also have a reversed meaning when they land facing down.

Instead of focusing on the specifics, you should concentrate on the aspects of life the runes may be related to. Each rune showcases principles, events, and influences from different areas of life. By showing up when they do, they're trying to get your attention. The runes send a message through your intuition each time they appear, so make sure you listen to it. Of course, being able to do that requires plenty of introspection. This is where the spiritual side of runic divination comes in. Being a driving force for your intuition, this divinatory practice helps organize your thoughts and emotions. Apart from making you more focused and productive in your day-to-day life, this also leads to spiritual elevation. It helps you become more aware of your needs and desires and encourages you to make them a reality. In addition, the answers you receive during runic deviation may reveal hidden motivations and behavior patterns that aren't aligned with your values. It certainly gives you plenty to reflect on. Even if you aren't interested in achieving specific goals with the runes, working with them can be beneficial for your mental health and spiritual well-being.

Rune Layouts

Once you have practiced reading runes and made a connection with them, you can try casting simple layouts. Below are several spreads you can try interpreting, starting from the easy three-rune layout and ending with the complex 24-rune reading.

The Three-Rune Layout

Also called the Three Norns, this cast is great for beginners because there are few runes to interpret. You don't need to learn complicated patterns, either. Here is how to do it:

1. Place three runes in a horizontal line. They should be facing upwards.

2. The first rune on the left will tell you what past actions resulted in your present situation.

3. The middle rune illuminates the issues you are currently dealing with, which will help you better understand your current situation.

4. The last rune represents the most likely future outcome based on your actions and current situation.

The Four-Rune Spread

The four-rune cast (or Four Dwarves) is another easy layout that works for simple readings. It uses a circular pattern, and you'll read the runes going clockwise. Here is how to interpret this layout:

1. Take a deep breath, select four runes from your pouch, and lay them out in a circle. One should be on top, two in the middle, and one on the bottom.

2. The top rune symbolizes past events that caused you to be in your current situation.

3. The left rune in the middle points out any influence other people have on your current situation.

4. The right rune in the middle alludes to the present actions that affect your current situation.

5. The bottom rune characterizes the full scope of your situation - often revealing hidden truths, motivations, or anything else you weren't aware of or couldn't admit to yourself.

The Five-Rune Layout

This cast is similar to the previous one, except you'll lay out the runes in the shape of a cross. It also uses two more symbols which means you may get a more in-depth answer to your questions. Here is how to cast it:

1. After relaxing, place five runes forming a cross. Start interpreting them from the bottom.

2. The rune at the base of the cross alludes to general influences related to your question.

3. The rune at the left horizontal side of the cross indicates the impact of negative forces related to the outcome in question.

4. The rune at the right horizontal side of the cross represents a short answer to your question.

5. The rune at the top of the cross hints at the positive energies that will impact the outcome.

6. The rune in the middle symbolizes any future actions that will impact the answer to your question.

The Seven-Rune Spread

When you gain confidence in reading simple layouts, you can move on to interpret more complex casts. The seven-rune cast can answer specific questions and reveal truths you weren't even aware of. Here is how to cast it:

1. Take a deep breath, clear your mind, and lay out seven runes (face-up) in a V form. Start interpreting from the top left side.

2. The top left rune indicates past influences that may impact the answer to the question.

3. The second rune from the left illuminates how your current actions may affect the answer to the question.

4. The last rune on the bottom left alludes to future influences that may impact the answer to the question.

5. The rune at the bottom of the V points to the actions you should take to reach the desired outcome.

6. The first rune on the right side at the bottom indicates any emotions that may impact your actions.

7. The rune above the previous one indicates any challenges related to the question.

8. The rune in the highest position on the right side represents the most likely future result related to your questions.

Nine-Rune Cast

In Norse mythology, nine is the number that holds answers to a lot of questions. This cast uses nine runes, but you won't have to worry about laying them out in a specific pattern. You'll just toss them out and see where they land. Here is how to cast and interpret runes with this method:

1. Take a deep breath and reach into your rune bag or box while focusing on your question.

2. Take out nine runes and place them in your dominant hand.

3. Closing your eyes, scatter the runes in front of you

4. Open your eyes and observe the positions of the runes after landing.

5. See how many runes are facing up and how many have landed face down. The latter indicates problems you weren't aware of. Despite this, they may affect your future. The ones facing you are influences you were already aware of.

6. Take a look at the runes that landed close to the center of the surface you're working on - these are the most important influences you need to focus on. The ones closer to the edge are less important but should not be disregarded either.

The 24-Rune Layout

Also called the Runic Year, this spread is typically used for long-term planning. Casting at the beginning of the year allows you to see an entire year's worth of influences and possible events and issues you may face in the coming year. It requires a bit more preparation in terms of cleansing - and you'll need to focus more as there is a lot more information to interpret. Here is how to cast this spread:

1. Lay out the 24 runes in a 3x8 grid, and start reading from the right side of the first row.

2. The first rune in the first row indicates the ways you'll obtain financial gains and prosperity.

3. The second rune represents the ways you can attain physical health and fitness.

4. The third rune shows how you'll defend yourself or destroy any issues on your way.

5. The fourth rune hints towards obtaining wisdom and motivation to keep going.

6. The fifth rune illuminates the direction of your life's path as seen under the current influences.

7. The sixth rune represents the knowledge you'll gain through the year.

8. The seventh rune shows what skills you can develop and hone and the gifts you'll receive.

9. The last rune in the first row alludes to how you'll obtain peace, harmony, and joy in your life.

10. The first rune on the right side of the second row indicates future changes that may await you.

11. The second rune represents the action you must take to obtain the desired results.

12. The third rune will show any obstacles that may hinder you on your journey.

13. The fourth rune indicates success and achievements you'll gain throughout the year.

14. The fifth rune alludes to challenging situations and choices you'll need to make to overcome them.

15. The sixth rune illuminates the inner skills that you need to work on.

16. The seventh rune symbolizes crucial life situations you'll find yourself in.

17. The last rune of the second row brings forward the inner energy that'll guide you.

18. The first rune on the right side of the third row represents legal and business affairs.

19. The second rune shows how you'll obtain prosperity and growth.

20. The third rune indicates the friendships and other relationships you'll form.

21. The fourth rune symbolizes your expected social status in the coming year.

22. The fifth rune alludes to the changes in your emotional state.

23. The sixth rune represents any romantic or sexual relationships you'll have.

24. The seventh rune shows how you'll obtain balance in all areas of life.

25. The last rune of the bottom row symbolizes all the assets you'll gain throughout the year.

Using Casting Boards

If you want answers to specific questions but aren't sure which cast would work the best, another option is to use a casting board. These are pre-made sheets or boards with areas of the present, past, future, and other crucial aspects of your life already laid out. All you need to do is toss the runes and look where they land. The ones that land in the past section will give you answers related to your past experiences. The ones landing in the present section are linked to your present, while the ones in the future will reveal what you should expect moving forward.

Chapter 9: Celtic Shamanism and Druidry

This chapter covers everything you need to know about Celtic Shamanism and Druidry. Here, you'll find out what each term means and understand the core beliefs of each practice. You'll understand the roles of shamans and druids and come across a section that illustrates the difference between both spiritual philosophies.

Druidic Ceremony for the Autumn Equinox on Primrose Hill in London, England.

Celtic Shamanism

Celtic Shamanism studies the spiritual beliefs and practices of ancient Irish, Welsh, Scottish, and some English people. Celtic people belonged to a large, diversified tribe that resided in the area around Germany and encompassed the French Gauls around the year 1500 BC.

Asia Minor was thought to be the origin of these indigenous tribes before they spread out toward eastern and western Europe, the Celtic Isles, and the Iberian peninsula. Ancient Celts were mostly known for their trading and mining skills. Germany's salt mines and France's gold mines largely contributed to their prominence and wealth.

These tribes were war-like yet open-minded. They had no problem taking over the lands they came across while traversing Europe. Still, they didn't mind being influenced by the artistic expressions and spiritual beliefs of others.

Shamanism isn't an organized religious tradition. It can be thought of as a way of life that requires you to journey your way into the spiritual realm and back so you can connect with your spirit guides and ask for their guidance on several matters, including healing and divination. There is no particular text that you can turn to when practicing Shamanism. It's important to understand that even though all practitioners share the same core beliefs, their shamanic practices, rituals, spiritual journeys, and experiences can greatly differ.

One of the core aspects of Shamanism is that its practitioners believe that everything around them has a spirit. They thought that the entire world was interconnected and that the spirit realm stimulated our world. Shamans trust that they can refer to the spiritual world whenever they need to ask for protection, wisdom, or healing. Even when Christianity made its way into Europe, people still believed that the divine was eminent in all aspects of nature.

Who Are Shamans?

A shaman is someone who journeys into the realm of the spirit as a proxy for wisdom and healing-related advice that would help them and those around them. Shamans had a broad range of skills that benefited the community in numerous ways.

For instance, a ban feasa/leighis, which translates to "woman of knowledge/healing," conducted healing rituals, broke evil spells, eliminated unwanted spirits, and offered healing remedies. The healing work of those who followed the faery faith was dedicated to the fae and inspired by it.

Omen hunters and seers traditionally conducted oracle work to inform people about the future. They also determined the wisdom behind some of the community's decisions and actions. Unlike the modern-day world, storytellers and poets were not regarded as entertainment figures but played significant societal roles. They were even regarded as healers. After all, art, in all its forms, is meant to leave an impact on our mental and emotional states.

A Shaman's Worldview

A shaman's worldview is characterized by its depth. They experience the world differently than we do because their perceptions are far more layered and analytical. They listen deeply and actively to everything around them. They're avid observers of nature and always live in the present moment. They don't concern themselves much with the past, and even though they are blessed with the gift of divination, they don't spend a lot of time worrying about the future. Shamans make the most of each moment that they're living, making it their mission to experience it with all their senses.

They acknowledge nature's beauty and express gratitude for everything they have. Being engrossed and attentive to nature and the current moment allows them to feel thankful for the things that we deem normal or insignificant. We get caught up in the dynamics of the everyday world that we take phenomena like the rising sun, streaming rivers, and animal produce for granted. Shamans, however, greet the sun each morning. They thank the plants and animals for sustaining them and honor them for keeping them warm and cooking their food. They end their day with a thankful prayer to nature.

Shamans garner their strength from this humbled, acknowledging, and thankful attitude. They realized that these simple gestures meant a lot to nature and the divine. Since they believed that spirit existed in everything, it was only appropriate for them to pay their respects and grant it their attention at all times.

A Celtic shaman's universe comprises three realms: the lower world, the middle world, and the upper world. They believed all of them were conjoined by the Tree of Life. This tree's roots are deeply planted into the lower world. Its trunk extends through the middle world, where we exist, and into the upper realm. The branches of this great tree are responsible for keeping the sun, the stars, and the moon up in the sky.

They believe that when they transcend into the realm of the divine, they climb up the tree or the great ladder. There resides the Great Mother goddess, deities, spirits, the stars, and other celestial bodies. They can also make their way into the lower realm by climbing down the roots of the tree where there are the spirits of fire and the earth and the horned one. He is the deity of the underworld and the protector of all animals.

Despite the size of the realms and the great Tree of Life, shamans believed that they all exist within a hazelnut shell that lies next to the source of all the wisdom in the world: the Well of Segais.

Celtic Shamans and Shapeshifting

Shapeshifting is another core aspect of the Celtic shamanic practice. This spiritual experience is essentially about the ability to simultaneously exist and partake in several realities. Shamans also believe that shapeshifting into another animal or living being allows them to draw on their healing and guiding powers. Their journey is considered incomplete if they're unable to move their consciousness into that of another being before returning.

Celtic Shamans and Totem Beasts

According to Celtic shamanic beliefs, everyone is protected by a totem beast that accompanies them on their life journey at the time of birth. This totem animal can stay with a person until they die. Shamanic practitioners obtain other power animals, in addition to their totem animals, at different times during their life. These animal guides may join a shaman at their own will or can be called upon for help. Sometimes, practitioners draw upon the animal's powers, whether it is their intuition, strength, sharp senses, or speed. In other cases, the animals tell the practitioner things they can't discern independently.

During the earlier years of human existence, animals and humans were much closer on several levels than they are today. We used to live in closer proximity to animals, and there was a higher level of mutual understanding. As the world grew more modernized, we fell out of touch with nature and the animal kingdom. Shamans, however, are keen on maintaining strong relationships with animals because numerous spirits represent them in the world of the divine.

Druidry

There are prominent similarities between Wicca and Paganism. However, it's important to remember that Druidism is not a subset of Wicca. Some Wiccans choose to practice Druidism, too, because of the similarities they share. The majority of Druids, however, are not Wiccan.

There are few reliable written accounts about Druidry. Most of the information that modern practitioners know comes from Celtic lore, mythology, and legend. They also rely on the academic information offered by historians and anthropologists as it serves as a basis for their practices, rituals, and rites.

Druidry, like Shamanism, is a nature-based belief system. Although it is very similar to Wicca, it focuses more on nature and ancestry. Druidry doesn't have a scripture or a sacred book to turn to. This is why it can come in several forms and easily adapt to various spiritual beliefs. Many people don't realize that regardless of your faith, whether you're a monotheist, polytheist, animist, or pantheist, you can still adopt some aspects of the druid philosophy.

Monotheistic druids believe in a single deity, while polytheists affirm the deities. Animistic and pantheistic druids may not believe in the presence of a single God. However, they would still affirm his existence as a force that exists in everything around us.

Druidism is incredibly tolerant of various spiritual and philosophical beliefs. The best thing about it is that it teaches that no belief system is superior to another. It all depends on the path that the individual chooses to follow.

The following are the core elements of the Druid faith:

- Life is a journey. All the stages of life, such as birth, adulthood, marriage, children, and all the stages leading up to death, and death itself, create a journey.
- Druidry is a healing practice. Healing utilizes holistic methods to heal the mind, body, and spirit.

- Druidry is a magical practice. It involves the use of divination practices to foretell the future and allows us to manifest our ideas.

- Reincarnation is possible. Ancient druids believed in a type of reincarnation which involved the journeying of the soul to the Otherworld before its reincarnation. This was taught in both animal and human forms and is still held onto by some modern practitioners.

- Each person must unlock their potential. Unlocking our potential is necessary if we wish to develop our intuitive, creative, intellectual, and psychic powers.

- All life is sacred. All life is equally valuable and sacred and withholds aspects of divinity. Animals, plants, and humans are all of the same levels of importance.

- We need to be in touch with nature. Practicing Druidry keeps us aligned with our ancestors, natures, and, ultimately, ourselves.

- There is an Otherworld. There is an otherworld that we will transcend to when we die. Although this place exists beyond our consciousness, it can be accessed via visualization, meditation, or other techniques that trigger a trance state.

Even though Christianity replaced Druidry in the 7th century, some British people found inspiration in this philosophy during the 18th century. There was very little information about ancient sages and practitioners; however, this spiritual practice was somehow rekindled. It didn't take long before other scholars around Europe also found the subject appealing.

Those who take up an interest in Druidry are often individuals who grow discontented with conventional belief systems. They wish to build a deeper connection with their ancestors and the earth on which they live. People who seek comfort in Druidry are those who wish to feel rooted and grounded in an incredibly fast-paced world. Druidry, for many people, serves as an anchor.

Who Are Druids?

A druid can be loosely defined as a member of the educated ancient Celtic society. They took up various societal roles, including teaching, priesthood, and acting as judges. Many of them were also scientists and philosophers. They seldom recorded their activities, so very little information about them is known.

Druids were considered the official arbitraries of justice and the truth because they studied moral philosophy. They were trusted enough to make decisions that would serve the greater good of society. They preached the concepts of the afterlife and the existence of an Otherworld. Druids developed solar and lunar calendars and studied the movement of celestial objects. Their understanding of the world prompted their celebration of the 8 annual Sabbats, which were seasonal celebrations.

It would take someone around 20 years of studying to become a druid. All the information they needed to know was transmitted orally. Since there were no books or notes to study, the whole learning process relied on memory.

Their role in the community was similar to that of priests now. They aimed to help people build a connection with the divine. Druids were highly esteemed members of the community. Their powers didn't only encompass spiritual practices, but they also had authority over the public. They were able to banish those who failed to conform to sacred laws. The Druids were powerful enough to call off wars. They didn't have to become army men, nor were they charged tax payments either. Druid women were equally esteemed and rightful. They were able to call their marriages off and serve in the army if they desired.

Julius Caesar, one of the primary sources of information about the Druids, explained that the Druids executed public and private sacrifices. They mainly sacrificed criminals for those who fell very ill or were in danger of dying in battle. However, they would sometimes sacrifice innocent individuals if the situation called for it.

They also advised those who went to them for guidance, judged all quarrels in the community, and decreed appropriate penalties. Caesar recounted that those who failed to meet the decree were exempted from sacrifice, which was thought to be a harsh punishment. The Druids appointed a chief, who was replaced upon death. They voted between candidates if there were several equally qualified ones. That said, they often thought that they wouldn't be able to come to a satisfactory resolution without armed violence.

The Bards

Bards were responsible for keeping and reinforcing traditions. They were thought to be the protectors of the world's sacredness. They weren't as thoroughly educated as Druids, as they likely only completed the first level of apprenticeship training. That said, they weren't at all thought to be inferior to Druids.

Bards could achieve different levels of accomplishment. Of course, the most proficient ones were treated with the highest regard. They also filled in several roles of the Druid and the Ovate. Ovates were mainly seers and diviners but were also possibly midwives, herbalists, and healers.

Training as a Bard was not an easy feat. It was a challenging and lengthy process that took around 12 years.

Celtic Shamanism vs. Druidry

Both shamans and druids were highly respected members of society. Shamans were considered diviners, healers, and proxies between the human world and the spiritual realm. Druids were regarded as diviners, healers, political advisors, and religious leaders. While modern-day practitioners of both philosophies have the same skill sets, they contribute to society differently.

The main difference between Shamanism and Druidry is that the former can be described as a worldview or approach, while the latter is considered a religion for many people.

The word "shaman" has recently evolved to describe any person who interacts with the world of spirit despite their faith or religion. The Druidic philosophy, however, is a nature-oriented spiritual system. This means that a person can be a Druid or a shaman. Even if they're not necessarily practitioners of Celtic Shamanism, they may supplement their druidic practices with shamanic activities and rituals.

Here's a rundown of the core beliefs of both practices:

- Animism is among the core aspects of Shamanism. Practitioners believe that each entity in nature has a spirit that you can interact with. While some of them are quite helpful, others are malicious. Druids are also animists. This nature-centered practice revolves around believing that nature has its own divine spirit.

- Shamans believe in a non-ordinary reality, which is the existence of another realm for the spirits. They embark on shamanic journeys to transcend into the world of spirit for various reasons, including holistic healing and divination.

- Shamans think that 3 realms make up an extraordinary world. Druids believe in the existence of a similar place (particularly to the upper world): the Otherworld. Since they believe in an afterlife, they think this is where humans go after death. However, this place can also be accessed by inducing a trance state or with the help of meditation.

- Shamans and druids both believe in interconnection. They think that all living beings are connected and are, therefore, in touch with the world of spirit.

Celtic Shamanism and Druidry have numerous aspects in common. While both of these philosophies share, more or less, the same core beliefs, they are not mutually exclusive. Celtic Shamanism is considered a methodology or approach. It has expanded to take on a broader meaning. Anyone who interacts with the world of spirit, regardless of their religion, is now regarded as a shaman by many.

Druidry, on the other hand, is more of a religion or belief system. That said, it is very tolerant of various spiritual and philosophical beliefs. It can also be adapted to numerous faiths, whether the practitioner is monotheistic, polytheistic, or animistic. There aren't many reliable written accounts about Druidry. Most of what we know comes from Julius Caesar's accounts, Celtic lore, and mythology. This is perhaps because the Druid learning process relied on memory and the oral transmission of information.

Chapter 10: Walking the Druid Path

In this chapter, you'll find out how you can become a druid and what it means to be one. You'll also learn everything you need to know about practicing Druidry in today's world. Finally, you'll find an exercise that can help you enrich your Druidic experience as a new practitioner.

Many druids commit to this spiritual path by going off the grid.

How Can One Become a Druid?

Druidry is essentially a journey of a deep, observant relationship with everything you encounter. Every day, we come in contact with nature, people, and animals. Some people come in contact with other unworldly entities too. However, suppose we're talking about the terrestrial plane. In that case, we deal with the land and other living beings and how we fit into this complex. Becoming a druid in ancient times took around 20 years. However, modern druids now believe that one can get into this belief system by growing their awareness and learning to be fully present in the current moment.

Understanding how your life positively and negatively contributes to the balance and well-being of the ecosystem is a great step forward. Druidry is a nature-centered religion, which is why druids try to keep their carbon footprint as small as possible. While avoiding all environmentally harmful activities in today's world is impossible, you should always seek less damaging and greener alternatives.

Many druids commit even further to this spiritual path by going off the grid. They grow their own food, engage in recycling and composting activities, make their own tools or clothes, and purchase second-hand items. Some believe that the world is overpopulated, so they refuse to have children.

Those who don't live off the grid try their best to make appropriate and good use of technology. They try to positively influence the community in which they live by promoting helpful, sustainable, ethical, and honorable practices.

One person may decide to completely boycott carbon-fueled transportation by choosing to walk or bike instead. They resort to modern means of transportation only if they really need to. Another person may think that living like that doesn't suit their lifestyle. They may work far from home, travel frequently, or run several errands a day. In that case, a druid will aim to use technology as mindfully as possible. They understand the consequences that come with technological advancements but still realize that avoiding these improvements isn't practical in today's fast-paced world. Despite their different approaches, each individual has an aware, personal, and mindful relationship with the world around them. Neither person is a better druid than the other.

There isn't a particular strict code or detailed guide to live by. Druidry adapts to various living conditions and rapid technological and societal changes. Each druid leads a unique life and practices their faith in a way that feels true to them. While not all druids have the same way of life, the core elements and beliefs of Druidry unify them.

Connections and Values

Practitioners are always on an ongoing quest to cultivate a deep spiritual bond and empathetic connections with their direct environment, the world, the entire universe, and all realities. They often find their deities where they least expect them, get to know their names, and build a transcendental, deep relationship with them. Each person comes in contact with their gods differently because there are almost no written records of ancient Druid practices. Most of what we know today is based on trial and error, intuition, and generational telltales. This is why any relationship that a person builds with a deity is incredibly personal. No one can tell you how to go about your faith or how to believe. You must lean into your intuition and do whatever feels right to you.

To be a druid, for many, is to have a voice and be heard. Many people use their faith as an opportunity to stand up for their principles and what they think is right. Most druids participate in eco-protest and activism-related activities. They always try to create positive changes in the world and contribute to a better living environment for all living beings.

Druidry is a vivacious and celebratory religion. It is ritualistic and connection-based. It's important that in your strife to build strong connections with the Earth and the realm of the spirits, you don't forget to cultivate equally deep relationships with those around you. If there's a Druid community in your area, don't pass up on the opportunity to meet up with them during celebrations, rituals, and even casual meet-ups. If there aren't any Druids nearby, you should still aim to interact with people who share the same values and interests. You can join clean-ups, charity events, and other volunteer work.

Awen

Awen can either be chanted silently within the soul or out loud. It comprises 3 sounds:

1. Ah makes you feel purposeful, incites joy, and promotes creativity and power.

2. Oo enlarges and maintains the power and energy that you have embraced, encouraging it to flourish.

3. Enn brings the whole process to an end. It builds boundaries and serves as a containment. It paves the way for everything that ah and oo have inspired and instigated.

Learning how to open yourself up to Awen is not a challenging feat. Pretend it's a window- how would you let all the natural air and light in? You'll probably approach the window, unhinge its latch, and open it wide. That's the only thing you need to do to let the sunshine, wind, and fresh air flow inside. They do all the work for you: light up your home, renew the air inside, and cool down and freshen up the room. You just sit back and watch it all unfold. It's exactly the same with Awen. You only need to take the first step to open it up and embrace it so you can allow it to do its thing without any interference.

Druidry lives up to the magic of the term itself. It encourages everyone who practices any art form to work in harmony to celebrate the Awen. Awen is a term that celebrates spirit, vitality, inspiration, and energy.

Reading into fables, parables, and telltales like the Mabinogion and the Tales of Taliesin can give you insight into the heritage of Druidry. You can learn about how people communicated with deities, related to them, celebrated them, and worked with them to achieve certain purposes pre-Druidry. You'll come to see that despite the fact that other spiritual beliefs influenced it with stories that have been recorded for hundreds of years, Druidry was unique because of how it allowed practitioners to adapt it to their needs. It never becomes dated because each generation revamps it to fit the standards of their world by keeping the core value intact. Its oral nature allows for a sense of continuity over the ages.

In a Nutshell

The question still stands- "How do you become a Druid?"

If you want to become a Druid, you must make peace with the fact that there is no solid answer to this question. While Druidry comes with no sacred book that you can turn to for guidance, there are many things you can do to build your own identity as a Druid. Reading books, such as this one, getting to know other Druids, partaking in rituals, connecting with nature, understanding the core beliefs of Druidry, reaching out to the divine and your spirit guides, learning how to become nature-centered, and most importantly, leading with your personal morals and values are all things that can help you out.

You may wonder at which stage of your practice it becomes okay to identify as a Druid. You must realize that no matter how much knowledge you have, you'll never know everything there is to know about this belief system- there is always something to learn. In other words, becoming a self-identified Druid is not necessarily tied to the amount of information you have obtained. Instead, it has to do with how deeply connected you are to the divine and the belief itself. Once you feel like you can formulate your own (non-judgmental) opinions on other people's practices and Druidic way of life, you'll be able to build your own identity as a practitioner.

Modern Druidry

The basics of Druid practices are shared by all practitioners and serve as a good foundation for developing personal practice-related standards, beliefs, morals, and ethics. Modern Druids are encouraged to seek the truth above all else.

Druidry today differs significantly from ancient practices, particularly because most of what we know today is based on observations, generational stories, and archaeological evidence and interpretations. Back then, practitioners didn't have access to as much information and tools as we do today, which is why their practices were purely experimental. However, nowadays, we have scholastic proof of natural phenomena, which further authenticates the Druidic experience. While many aspects of the belief system remain purely spiritual and intuitive, others have become fact-based. This makes Druidry more relatable and easier to wrap one's head around, especially for those who are still new to the practice. That said, many people prefer to turn a blind eye to the facts when it comes to spiritual beliefs and religion. They feel it's only right to let their intuition, the universe, and their spirit guides steer them toward the truth.

Roman recounts of ancient Druidic practices are highly illegal and unacceptable in today's world. Human sacrifices, for instance, is an activity that raises numerous questions. Did they sacrifice innocent people or execute dangerous criminals? It is believed that they were popular for keeping the heads of their enemies as trophies. Was this a sacrificial act or a prideful practice? Regardless of the truth behind this gruesome practice, human sacrifice is insufferable in today's world.

Upon exploring ancient Druidic practices, you could easily tell that everything they did was aligned with their time. They were exposed to numerous cultures and traditions and had to settle on trade agreements. They were also entangled in political issues, as they served as advisors to the rulers. They also healed the ill using more advanced tools and medical techniques than the Romans were capable of- they were truly ahead of their time! Druids helped their communities in numerous aspects, serving as teachers, judges of the truth, lawmakers, and ritual leaders, and advocated for great causes. They also promoted positive practices and social and environmental welfare and acted as counselors and spiritual service providers.

Modern Practices

Most Druids today are polytheistic. They believe in the existence of various deities, which mainly belong to the Welsh or Irish pantheons. The majority of practitioners work with Celtic pantheons. However, some groups believe that it's fine to follow whichever Indo-European pantheon they see fit, including Norse, Russian, and Germanic ones. It's commonly believed that some deities are not meant to be worked with for specific purposes. They'll choose the right god or goddess to work with, depending on the situation at hand. They often refer to a correspondence chart to ensure that they make the right choice. While many pagans worship a different deity each week, druids don't believe in this practice. This is because many pagan belief systems view all deities as a subset of a single divine figure, while Druids think each deity has its own individual identity. Since Druidry can be adapted to each person's faith, some Christians are also druids who believe in a single god. Others believe in no deities at all. They just adopt Druidry as mere philosophy.

One of the best things about Druidry is that it's open to everyone. It doesn't matter what your faith or ethnicity is. You are always welcome to explore Druidic practices. It's worth mentioning, however, that some modern druids choose to be very exclusive with their rituals and Druidic practices. They'll want to get to know you before they let you in on their spiritual activities.

Magic workings are not an essential aspect of Druidic practices. Wiccans prefer to practice magic because they view it as an opportunity to sharpen their skills. It is, more or less, a major part of their spiritual practice. However, many modern Druids never cast spells, and this doesn't make them any less of a true druid. Since nature is a quintessential part of Druidry, Neo-druids always do their best to choose more environmentally-friendly options.

There are 8 popular seasonal Pagan festivals: Samhain, Yule, Imbolc, Ostara, Beltane, Litha, Lughnassadh, and Mabon. However, only 4 of them are actually Celtic: Samhain, Imbolc, Beltane, and Lughnassadh. Even though many Druids like to celebrate all Sabbats or festivals, most of them choose to celebrate only the 4 main Celtic ones. Keep in mind that some druids are also part of spiritual groups that require them to celebrate all 8 Sabbats.

Modern druids aim to serve their needs, community, and deities by partaking in community services and volunteer work. They also practice ecological awareness, make environmentally-friendly decisions, strive to maintain balance in all aspects of their lives, and maintain respectful and consistent spiritual practices. Individuals who only view Druidry as a philosophy tend to approach their personal religions with a Druid approach.

Enrich Your Druidic Experience

Here are some things you can do to enrich your Druidic experience, even if you're still just starting out:

Go Outside

Disconnect from technology for a day and go outside. Go for a walk in a nature-dense place and find a quiet place to stay in. If you live in the city, visit your local park. This will not be like any other walk you've had- it is a walk with a purpose. Think about the last walk you had. What were you thinking about? Your mind was probably busy with thoughts about your to-do list, financial problems, family issues, or work. Leave your baggage behind for this walk. Only focus on the present moment and fully engage in the experience.

Observe

Once you find your quiet place, you must refine your senses. Extend your arms to your sides, creating the shape of a T. Look straight, right above the horizon, while moving your arms back. Move your fingers around while moving your arms forward again. Keep your arms still but allow your fingers to wiggle when they come into your peripheral vision. Keep looking straight ahead. This is something known as Wide Angle Vision. Once you see your fingers while your arms are extended to your sides, slowly drop your arms down while keeping your attention on everything around you.

Hear

Move your hands again and place them behind your ears. You'll be using them to control your hearing. Keeping your hands behind your ear can help you hear things more effectively. Focus on what you can hear better. Stay in this position for a while before moving your hands away. Listen to everything around you. You'll likely hear layers of sound that you didn't know you could hear. Listen mindfully, and then try to combine this exercise with the "observe" one.

Smell

Take some grass from the ground and crunch it in your palms. Take several sniffs in short, quick bursts, and avoid taking long ones. You can also try doing this exercise with soil or tree twigs around you. Try sniffing the air in short and quick bursts, as well. Then, combine this exercise with the heart and observe. Focusing on all three senses simultaneously can be very challenging. However, you'll master it through practice.

Each Druid decides how they will put their spiritual beliefs into practice. However, all modern-day practitioners can agree on the importance of living up to a certain level of integrity at all times. They also actively seek their personal truth through embarking on their own educational journeys, learning from other people, ritualistic practices, connecting with nature, and meditating.

Appendix: A-Z of Pagan Symbols

Pagan traditions are full of symbolism. This chapter serves as an appendix for the most used and significant ancient and modern symbols.

Aegishjalmur

This symbol is also known as the Helm of Awe. It is the epitome of safety and power, and its symbol resembles a circle that includes 8 staves. Fafnir, Hreidmar's son, carried this symbol with him when he fought Siegfried in the form of a dragon. Even though most of the dragon's power came from the Helm of Awe, Siegfried won the battle before taking the Aegishjalmur for himself.

Viking warriors used to draw this emblem on their foreheads because they believed it would strike fear in the hearts of their enemies and help protect them in battle. Besides being a protective symbol, the Helm of Awe was also thought to boost one's mental and physical strength.

Ankh

This is perhaps the most renowned ancient Egyptian emblem. It is popularly known as the Key of Life and was adopted in Paganism and Christianity as an emblem of the afterlife, eternity, life, and rebirth. Christians started using this symbol in the 4th and 5th AD after Egypt's partial Christianization.

Air

According to alchemy, air is one of the 4 basic elements on Earth. Pagans adopted the Alchemical symbol of air, which is an upward-facing triangle with a horizontal line cutting through its upper half. Since air is a necessity for human existence, it serves as an emblem of all life-giving forces and the soul itself. Pagans typically include it in spiritual practices and rituals.

Earth

The alchemical symbol of Earth is a downward-facing triangle with a horizontal line cutting through its lower (pointed) half. It symbolizes mother nature and is an emblem of physical movements, fertility, abundance, and nature.

Eye of Horus

Horus was the ancient Egyptian god of healing and protection. His eye was particularly known to be a protective symbol. It was believed to be extremely powerful, and ancient Egyptians trusted it would keep them safe in life-threatening situations. They sent it off with fishermen to protect them from the raging seas and buried it with those who had passed or drew it on their coffins to keep them safe on their journey to the afterlife. The pagans added the Eye of Horus to their symbols and incorporated the correspondent ancient Egyptian traditions into their lives.

Fire

The alchemical symbol of fire is a regular, upward-facing triangle. Fire is believed to be the embodiment of masculinity. Even though it can be destructive, it is also a life-supporting force since we need it to stay warm and cook food. Fire is also a symbol of intense emotions, like love, passion, and anger.

Hecate's Wheel

This symbol is the emblem of the Hecate. She is the Greek deity of magic and the moon. This wheel is representative of the Triple Goddess' three aspects, which are representative of the different phases in a woman's life. Each of them has distinct Wiccan practices. Pagans use this symbol to attract prosperity. Since the emblem is in the shape of a labyrinth, it is also believed to symbolize renewal and rebirth.

Mjolnir

Mjolnir, which is known as Thor's hammer in pop culture, is another Norse pagan symbol. Thor, the god of thunder, is among the most prominent Norse mythology figures. It was believed that when Thor threw Mjolnir, it always hit the right target and came flying right back to him. Viking warriors wore the symbol on necklaces because it was associated with protection. Thor's hammer remained a significant aspect of Norse culture even after the emergence of Christianity. Mjolnir is also popular among those who follow the neopagan religion of Asatru. Pagans even used the symbol to bless marriages.

Ouroboros

Depicted as a snake eating its own tail, Ouroboros is also known as the infinity symbol. This emblem is significant to various cultures, making it among the most important symbols to the entirety of humankind. Cleopatra the Alchemist (not Egypt's Ptolemaic ruler) is considered to be the first to use this symbol. Her works date back to the 3rd Century BC.

Cleopatra featured the Ouroboros in a work that revolved around the mythical philosopher's stone, which was thought to turn any metal into pure gold. Many alchemists used the infinity symbol to represent life, death, and rebirth, which is the unending cycle of life. It was also associated with Mercury, the chemical element, rebirth, and reincarnation. The Ouroboros also represents the harmony and duality of two opposing forces or sides.

Pentacle

A pentacle is a five-pointed star enclosed in a circle. According to pagan beliefs, circles symbolize power and infinity. In that case, the circle in the Pentacle reinforces the power of the five-pointed star. It also reflects the interconnectedness of earth, air, water, fire, and spirit. Pagans use this emblem for protection in their practices.

Pentagram

This symbol looks exactly like a pentacle. However, it isn't enclosed in a circle. The 5 points of the star represent the 4 basic elements plus the spirit.

Septogram

The Septogram is a seven-pointed star. The symbol is also known as the faery star, heptagram, and septagram. Besides Paganism, this emblem is significant in other faiths, like Christianity and Islam, across the globe. Christians use it as an emblem for the creation of the world, which took 7 days, while Muslims use it to symbolize the Quran's first 7 verses. The heptagram in Paganism is associated with numerous concepts that come in 7s. For example, it was used to represent 7 ancient classical planets and the Seven Sisters or Pleiades, which were thought to be the titan Atlas' daughters.

Svefnthorn

Norse witches and magicians used the Svefnthorn to induce sleep among their subjects. This symbol was also known as the Sleep Thorn, and its depiction differs from one source to the other.

The Horned God

The Horned God represents masculinity, hunting, and sexuality. It is symbolized by a circle that has an upward-facing crescent on top of it. It's used in Wiccan invocation rituals, particularly ones that have to do with fertility.

The Sacred Spiral

The Sacred Spiral was prominently used among ancient Celts and pagans. It symbolizes the Goddess and is associated with life, death, and rebirth. The Sacred Spiral also represents the movement of celestial objects in the sky and the everlasting nature of things.

The Sun Wheel

The Sun Cross, or the Sun Wheel, is a pagan symbol that symbolizes the sun. It represents lids, immortality, fertility, and life-granting forces. The Sun Wheel also depicts the Eight Sabbats of Wicca and the four seasons of the year.

The Tree of Life

This symbol carries great meaning for several ancient civilizations, including that of the Celts. According to Norse Mythology, this ash tree was thought to serve as a bridge for the Nine Realms. Trees and nature, in general, are very important to Celtic practitioners, which is why tribes chose to settle near trees and meet under them.

The Triple Horn of Odin

Trinities are highly pronounced in pagan traditions, and the Triple Horn of Odin is no exception. This symbol, which is also known as the horned triskele, is made up of three horns joined together to create what looks like a triangle. It is believed to illustrate the 3 times that Odin, the god of war and death, drank the mystical wisdom and poetry mead, which was thought to be made of the blood of a wise god. Horns were mentioned several times in the Manuscripts of the Prose Edda, and Vikings typically used them to toast in ceremonies, as well. These are all things that make this symbol particularly significant to the pagan faith.

Water

Water is an important symbol used in pagan invocation practices and rituals. The alchemical symbol of water is the exact opposite of that of fire: an inverted triangle. The pagan symbol for water is associated with femininity and is representative of the womb. It is commonly used in love rituals, as well as purification and cleansing ones.

Conclusion

As one of the oldest religions in the world, Paganism has an incredibly rich history. Learning about its background and evolution can be a great stepping stone if you want to develop any type of Pagan practice. This book has introduced you to the lives of the ancient Pagans - including their beliefs and their fight to maintain them when pressured by other religions. You've also learned that Paganism encompasses a wide range of practices and has once dominated the beliefs of the entire world's population. While nowadays it is less commonly practiced, anyone can embrace the Pagan path, regardless of their cultural or religious background.

Paganism is a spirituality-based religion, an aspect that helps followers understand and develop their practices. At the core of the belief system is a reverence for several gods and goddesses, all believed to impact a certain aspect of life. The deities are also linked to natural elements, which is in accordance with the other crucial dogma in Paganism - the veneration of nature. Nature and the gods are celebrated through different festivities like the equinoxes, representing a significant turning point in nature and people's lives.

Contemporary practices have held onto some of the ancient traditions, although some only in a very rudimentary form. Others have incorporated elements from other religions mainly due to the pressure of assimilation and survival. Neopaganism and Wicca (one of the newest Pagan religions) are both inspired by ancient magic practices. The latter represents an entirely new form of the spiritual path. If you feel that this path answers your spiritual needs, the chapter about its practical use can help you implement it into your practices.

The form of Paganism you've learned about in this book is Norse Paganism. While Wiccans rely on magical practices to reach spiritual goals, Norse Pagans have a high reverence for the afterlife and their ancestors. In Norse beliefs, ancestors are considered to be just as powerful guides as the deities are. Modern Norse Pagan practices incorporate rites of passage, festivals, and plenty of other acts you can perform - just as those who walked the old Norse Seidrs path did. These ancient shamanic practitioners were the masters of journeying and trance, through which they accessed all kinds of information.

The most common way to access information is through the Norse runes. Apart from being the letters of an ancient alphabet, runes are also unique divinatory tools with magical powers that reveal future events. The runes are divided into three major groups called Aetts - which hold the key to a specific set of information in the practitioner's subconscious. Their use requires learning about their symbolism but also highly developed intuitive skills.

Last but not least, you've learned about the connection between Celtic Shamanism and Druidry - two practices that, in ancient times, were held in high regard. Both Shamans and Druids were highly trusted members of Celtic societies. Yet nowadays, their roles have taken a divergent path through history. While shamans retained their healing practices, druids started to veer towards the patronage of arts, history, and philosophy. Despite this, Druids remain one of the most mysterious practitioners of Paganism. However, as you've learned from the book, if you choose to walk the Druid path, there are plenty of ways to do it.

Part 2: Celtic Shamanism

The Ultimate Guide to Celtic Druidry, Spirituality, Earth Magic, Spells, Symbols, and Tree Astrology

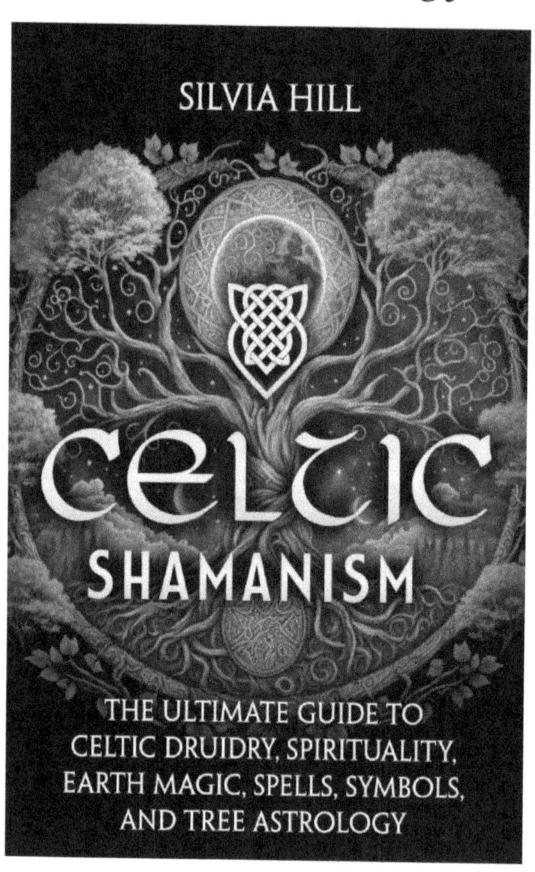

Introduction

The Celtic people are one of the oldest cultures in the British Isles. Much of it survives to this day through the modern cultures of those living in Ireland, Scotland, Wales, and parts of England. The Gaelic, Cornish, Welsh, Breton, Manx, and Scottish Gaelic languages are all considered part of the Celtic family of languages, having evolved from the original Proto-Celtic language spoken by the ancient Celts. Their influence can be felt even beyond these languages - many of the customs, festivals, holidays, and religious practices of the people living in the British Isles can be directly linked back to the ancient Celtic culture.

The fascination many people have with the Celtic people stems from the way society developed from the classical to late medieval eras of history. This was a transitional period, as the native Celtic and Anglo-Saxon tribes living in the British Isles were first exposed to Continental European cultures through the invasion, conquest, and occupation carried out by the Roman Empire. Once they arrived, Christianity followed not long after. The strife between the Celtic and Roman people caused a significant shift in the characteristics of both cultures.

While Christianity became increasingly prominent, it became a standard procedure for missionaries to work toward assimilating the local populace with as little resistance as possible. They used this tactic in an attempt to adapt the deities, myths, and religious practices of the native peoples into existing Christian dogma. This process is known as syncretization, where the Christian angels, saints, and feast days are assigned an association with similar parts of the local religion. However, it wasn't a one-way street. Celtic paganism also adopted pieces of Christianity into their own belief system.

One of the few irreconcilable aspects of Celtic culture that Christianity refused to acknowledge were the roles of certain religious leaders, like shamans and Druids. Although superficially similar to priests, bishops, and cardinals, their practices and beliefs were incongruent with Christianity's viewpoint on souls, spirits, and magic. Shamans and Druids became increasingly irrelevant, becoming victims of Christian assimilation. For centuries afterward, they were effectively extinct, with only a few pockets of surviving Celtic pagans still possessing either one.

Fortunately, the neopagan revival and reconstruction of the ancient Celtic religion included the resurrection of shamans and Druids as respectable spiritual occupations. Their emphasis on preserving nature and encouraging people to live in harmony with existing ecosystems has become much more relevant as the subject of environmentalism is pushed to the forefront of societal responsibilities. Shamans and Druids set a positive example of how we can utilize natural resources without harming the environment. If their warnings are not heeded, there might not be much of a world left for future generations to inherit.

With thousands of years' worth of history behind it, the Celtic religion and culture is a very appealing subject to explore. Many aspects of Celtic society can teach you lessons applicable to the current age. When you start reading this guide, keep that fact in mind, and try to look at it through the lens of a 21st-century audience. Some parts of the ancient Celtic culture might seem far removed from the modern experience, but we have more in common with our ancestors than you might initially believe. If you immerse yourself in everything surrounding Celtic traditions, you will emerge with a much greater understanding of a people who can live harmoniously alongside nature without causing irreparable harm.

Chapter 1: The Roots of Shamanism

Shamanism is a religious practice involving mysticism and animism, with a heavy focus on the spiritual realm. Its roots extend back thousands of years and across many different cultures. This included the Celtic and Gaelic people in Ireland and Scotland, Native Americans in North America, the indigenous peoples of South America, and other pockets of select tribal cultures in Asia and Australia. Each developed its own brand of shamanism, but they all had a few key components in common that made them recognizable as the same basic practice.

Shamanism is a religious practice involving mysticism and animism.
https://unsplash.com/photos/89tJEmx3VuA

Basic Aspects of Shamanism

The concept of the spiritual realm and the spirits that inhabit it are considered by shamanism to be an important part of an individual's experience, as well as having a role in society at large. Spirits can be benevolent, malevolent, or a combination of both. Finding ways to communicate with these spirits is one of the primary functions of shamans, who are believed to be able to enter the spiritual realm and treat illnesses caused by malevolent spirits. Benevolent spirits are often consulted by a shaman when seeking answers to questions outside their own breadth of knowledge.

Part of shamanism includes using animal symbols and imagery, as animals are seen as spirit guides that assist people in overcoming obstacles in their lives. Sometimes, these animals can also serve as messengers from the spiritual realm or provide omens to forewarn the shaman of major events to come. Shamans can perform divination rituals to more actively discern the future, use runes or bones, and scry for hints about things beyond their ken. Sometimes, they can even induce trances to enter a state of ecstasy where they have visions or undertake a vision quest.

Shamanistic Beliefs

Shamanism's main belief is that an invisible spiritual realm exists alongside the physical world, where spirits of a wide variety dwell. It also maintains that there is a spiritual power within all living beings. However, the potency of this power is stronger in certain beings, such as humans or sacred animals. Learning how to identify these spirits and connect to the spiritual realm can allow a shaman to gain knowledge and power they would not otherwise be accessible.

The Soul

The soul is essentially the spirit contained within a living being, particularly a human. This is the part that continues on after death and enters the spiritual realm. Some forms of shamanism even believe that a person can possess two or more souls simultaneously. In these cases, one of the souls will always remain with the person's body, known appropriately as the "body soul." The others can leave the body at will and are called the "wandering souls." A shaman must have at least two souls to perform their duties, as they are sometimes required to send their wandering soul away from their body to enter the spiritual realm and commune with the spirits living there.

The Spirits

The spirits associated with shamanism are often seen in the form of humans or animals. The soul is believed to leave the body, either consciously while alive or unconsciously after death, and the soul is then transported to the spiritual realm. Some animals are also considered spirits, even in their physical bodies, due to their strong connection to the spiritual realm. Animals like eagles, wolves, jaguars, snakes, and rats are viewed as spirit animals by many shamanistic traditions, and using their actions and behaviors can assist a shaman in reading omens and determining the future.

Animism

Animism is the belief that everything in nature has its own spiritual representations with which a shaman can interact. This includes animals, trees, flowers, and plants and the elemental forces of fire, earth, water, and air. As with most spirits, these have the potential to be both good and evil, and a shaman can communicate with them directly. It requires a strong foundational understanding of how the world works in relation to the spirits for a shaman to successfully navigate the spiritual realm.

The Spiritual Realm

The spiritual realm is considered a non-ordinary reality, meaning it is an entirely separate and distinct world from ordinary reality. The spirit realm exists in the same physical space as the real world but is hidden by a veil that can only be pierced by shamans and other exceptional individuals. This is where all spirits dwell when they no longer possess a physical form. Those trained to walk among the spirits may send their souls to the spiritual realm to communicate with the spirits that reside there. While people cannot normally see the spirits living within the spiritual realm, they can see those in the physical world, watching events and learning secrets that they can pass along to shamans.

Most traditions maintain that the spiritual realm is divided into three tiers, the lower, middle, and upper levels. A spirit's position within this hierarchy is dependent on the amount of spiritual power they possess, with the most important dwelling within the upper level, while the least important are constrained to the lower level. The spirits of dead humans are generally seen in the middle level, as the lower one is reserved for the majority of animal spirits, and the upper level is designated for the most enlightened beings.

Interconnectivity

The majority of shamans believe that everything is fundamentally interconnected. The physical world and the spiritual realm are enmeshed in a way that precludes one from operating normally without the other. Some of it is seen as having a give-and-take relationship between the spirits and the shamans. Suppose someone is attempting to catch fish for their family to survive. In that case, a shaman might beseech the spirits to allow the fisherman to catch what they need. In return, the spirits are compensated for this boon through prayers and sacrifices. It is a holistic approach to the universe's mechanics, thriving on this interconnectivity and equal exchange of favors.

Healing Powers

Most shamans can use their connection to the spirits to heal the body, the mind, and the soul. It is believed that when a person becomes sick, one of the causes may be that their soul has strayed from their physical body, so a shaman must retrieve the missing soul and reunite it with the ailing person. In other instances, a shaman can appeal to the spirits to use their energy to help encourage healing within an injured person, speeding up their recovery time. When someone is having problems with their mind or soul, shamans can also communicate with the spirits to get advice on how to help them fix the person's troubles.

Fertility

Some shamanistic cultures believe that when a woman struggles with fertility issues, the cause may be due to the lack of a soul for the child she is trying to conceive. To remedy this situation, a shaman can visit the spiritual realm to locate the lost soul of the child and bring it back to their mother, thus solving the problem. Shamans also have the ability to ask the spirits about a potential future child, such as what their name should be or what their destiny could hold. When a woman is infertile and a shaman cannot find their child's soul, the shaman may be able to contact the spirits to discover why this has happened.

Hunting

When hunting game or other animals, there must be some sort of appeasement given to their souls when they are killed. This includes using shamans to communicate with the released souls of the animals and give them thanks for their sacrifice, as well as beseech them to speak to their living brethren, convincing them to allow themselves to be killed for the benefit of the hunter. As many shamanistic cultures view animals as both sacred and a source of food, they feel it is essential to ensure that they do not offend the spirits of the animals they slay. They make it clear that the killing is not made out of malice but out of necessity, which the animals usually understand.

The System of Shamanism

Shamanism has several different systems and practices that are included in their religion. To enter the spiritual realm, they must travel across the "axis mundi," or the hidden ley lines between the Earth's two poles. They bring about a state of extra-sensory consciousness by inducing an ecstatic trance, which can be achieved by ritual performances, autohypnosis - essentially hypnotizing themselves - or by using entheogens. Each shamanistic culture employs its own methods, but sometimes these practices can be used in conjunction.

Ritual Performances

The types of ritual performances a shaman can use to enter the spiritual realm often involve music and songs. Like the different forms of shamanism itself, the types of music and songs used are equally diverse. Sometimes, a shaman will imitate sounds from nature, including those made by animals, using onomatopoeias. They will put them in the form of a song, repeating certain significant sounds as a chorus to help them get into the state of mind to transcend their physical body. Other types of music and songs can be closer to those most people would find familiar, using instruments and traditional vocal singing, or even throat singing, as performed by many Inuit cultures. The purpose of these performances is to break free the shaman from the physical world, allowing their soul to enter the spiritual realm and commune with the spirits therein.

Autohypnosis

Autohypnosis is similar to meditation in that a person uses relaxation techniques and concentration of the mind to direct their thoughts and energy toward a specific goal. Shamans can do this as a means of entering the spiritual realm. They will separate themselves from all distractions and focus all their energy on sending their soul to commune with the spirits. When this is done successfully, a shaman can easily travel across the spiritual realm and gain insight and knowledge from those they meet. When they are finished, they can return to their body and snap themselves out of their hypnotic state.

Entheogens

An entheogen is a psychoactive substance (i.e., a drug) used to induce a heightened state of consciousness in which a shaman can cross over into the spiritual realm. Entheogen means "generating the divine within," so the idea is that through their use, a shaman is able to send their soul into the spiritual realm to connect with the spirits dwelling there. When used in a ritualistic context by experienced shamans, entheogens are not considered dangerous, as shamans have been trained to apply their effects safely. Entheogens can be substances like peyote, psilocybin mushrooms, uncured tobacco, salvia divinorum, iboga, cannabis, and ayahuasca. These are all-natural psychoactive substances. Synthetic drugs like LSD or ecstasy are not permitted for ritualistic purposes.

Shamanism around the World

Shamanism can be found in cultures worldwide, although each has its own variations that make them unique. Because it extends back so far in history, it is impossible to know whether shamanism began in one culture and spread to others through trade and war or if each brand of shamanism was developed independently. However, the fact that they all share common aspects speaks to the universal appeal of the religion, even in cultures that may look very different, as they all still hold to the belief of spirits and the spiritual realm existing alongside the physical world.

Africa

Shamanism in Africa can be found among the Dogon, the Sisala, the Zulu, the Nguni, and the Karanga people. Shamans are also often called "medicine men," and part of their duties include warding off evil spirits. Illnesses are thought to be the product of witchcraft, necessitating a shaman to counter the evil magic and heal the sick. Shamans can also be herbalists; they are needed to help maintain a balance within nature and keep people from suffering from the negative effects of disharmony between the living and the dead.

Asia

The Hmong people in China had professional shamans who used rituals and trances to bring harmony to individuals, families, and communities, preventing the environment from becoming hostile to them. In Japan, the Shinto and Ainu religions include shamanism, especially

Shinto, which promotes shamans as a major part of their agricultural societies. North and South Korea have shamans, although the male shamans are known as "baksoo mudangs," while the female shamans are called "mudangs." They are given their positions either through hereditary descent or by displaying natural shamanistic abilities. Cultures in Siberia, Mongolia, Malaysia, and the Philippines also have shamanistic traditions, where shamans are held in high regard.

India has several practices very similar to shamanism, although they use names like the "Nechung Oracle," which serves the same function as a shaman. Even the Dalai Lama consults the oracle for spiritual advice, and the Nechung Oracle is the official state oracle of the Tibetan government. In Nepal, shamans are known as "Jhakri," and the Sunuwar, Tamang, Limbu, Kami, Sherpa, Rai, Gurung, Lepcha, and Magar people all have Jhakri within their communities. The Jhakri are also influenced by the traditions of Tibetan Buddhism, Hinduism, Mun, and Bön.

The Americas

In North American indigenous cultures like the Native Americans and First Nations, traditional roles exist, such as mystics, lore-keepers, healers, medicine people, and singers that greatly resemble shamans. However, the actual term "shaman" has never been used to describe these religious figures, instead giving them unique terms in their own languages. Not all indigenous cultures have a religious figure who communicates with the spiritual realm, connecting the living members of the community to the spirits. Those with a variety of traditions and beliefs are associated with the role, but the commonalities between them are very similar to the duties of a traditional shaman.

Ancient Mesoamerican cultures, including the Mayas and Aztecs, had members of the priesthood who performed the traditional shamanistic role. The Mayas had a class of priests who were specifically tasked as shamans, maintaining a complex network that crossed the entire empire. They used divination, healing rituals, dream interpretation, astrology, and trances to communicate with spirits within the spiritual realm. The Aztecs had priests who performed a similar function, and one of the major gods of their pantheon was Tezcatlipoca, which meant "smoking mirror," who was a Pan-Mesoamerican shaman god with omnipotence and universal power.

South American cultures such as the Urarina of the Peruvian Amazon, the Santo Daime, and União do Vegetal religions, the Mapuche people of

Chile, the Aymara people, and the indigenous people of Tierra del Fuego all have variations of shamanistic traditions. The Urarina people, as well as the Santo Daime and União do Vegetal religions, use the entheogen called ayahuasca during shamanistic rituals as a primary aspect of their society, connecting to the spiritual realm to gain guidance from divine spirits. Their shamans are highly regarded members of society, aiding the people in finding their place in the world and fulfilling their destinies. The Urarina call their shamans "ayahuasqueros," and their ayahuasca brews have been said to be a cure-all for maladies from addiction to depression and even cancer.

There are tribes in the Amazon rainforest whose shamans also serve to manage the scarcity of ecological resources. As deforestation plagues the rainforest, they attempt to mitigate the damage by overseeing replanting efforts. There is a tribe known as the Waiwai who have members of the community called the "yaskomo." They are essentially shamans, performing "soul flights" for healing, consulting cosmological beings for advice, and sending their souls down into the depths of the river to gain the aid of divine beings dwelling there. A yaskomo is able to make contact with the earth, the sky, and the water.

The Mapuche have "machis," women who perform ceremonial rituals to ward off evil spirits, cure diseases, and control the weather and harvest yields. The Aymara have a "Yatiri" who heals both the body and the soul and serves the community through performing rituals for Pachamama. One aspect of their healing abilities comes through certain shamanistic practices that use plant alkaloids consumed during therapeutic sessions. They believe that balancing the mind and soul makes it easier to mend the body.

In Tierra del Fuego, the indigenous people known as the Fuegians had a hunter-gatherer culture. Still, their religious practices were not homogenized across all the tribes. The Selk'nam and Yámana people were two Fuegian tribes that had shamanistic roles within their cultures. They believed their shamans had supernatural abilities, could control the weather, and communicate with their gods and other divine beings. The shamans also performed sacred rituals to help their hunters find and kill game animals for food and other rituals to aid with the foraging of resources and supplies.

Modern Latin American and some Spanish-based communities in the United States have a figure known as a "curandero," who specializes in both Western and traditional medicine, using techniques from both to help treat the physical, mental, emotional, and spiritual illnesses that can afflict their people. The Catholic Church also influences their form of shamanism. The curanderos will use traditional shamanistic methods combined with Catholic rituals or rites, including prayers, holy water, and religious imagery, to assist in their duties.

Europe

Across Eastern, Western, and Southern Europe, shamanism has a long tradition dating back to the ancient pre-Christian cultures in the region. In Italy, there was an agrarian cult known as the Benandanti, which had shamans that induced trances where they combated witches in a spiritual battle to save their people's crops. Many Germanic peoples had shamans tied closely with their warriors and magical beliefs. A type of warrior known as "berserkers" used trance-inducing rituals to send them into a frenzied state where they could fight without feeling pain. These practices were administered or overseen by a tribe's shaman leaders.

Shamanism in Northern Europe

In Northern Europe, the Nordic people were heavily influenced by the beliefs and practices of the pre-Christian Germanic cultures. They had a role called a Völva that acted as a shaman, offering guidance and spiritual advice to the members of their culture. The Welsh had soothsayers and prophets called the "awenyddion," who gave ominous prophecies in a deep trance in response to those seeking them for divine guidance. When an awenyddion was sought out for their expertise, it was customary to bring a token or gift to serve as an offering that could be used to help the awenyddion draw a stronger connection to the divine powers while in their trance.

Shamanism has long been associated with Gaelic traditions in Ireland and Scotland. Many tales and historical accounts include shamanistic aspects within Celtic cultures. Shamans are associated with heroes and leaders, usually taking an advisory role and utilizing their connection to the spiritual realm to gain knowledge of secrets and future events. This is particularly true with the stories involving King Arthur, where Merlin exhibits many traits of a shaman. The figures that Merlin is believed to be based on, Myrddin and Ambrosius, can similarly be viewed as shamanistic due to their prophetic abilities and connection to the spiritual realm. There is a rich history of shamanism in Celtic society, which has continued to the present day.

Chapter 2: What Is a Celtic Shaman?

Celtic shamanism has its roots in the British Isles, where it is believed to have been practiced by ancient indigenous cultures and early settlers. In Ireland, the Gaelic people native to the island had societal roles that were very clearly shamanistic. There was also a strong shamanistic component to the West Germanic tribes known as the Angles, Saxons, Frisians, and Jutes, who arrived in southern England following the withdrawal of the Roman invaders, while some of the Celtic Britons who already dwelt in the region and had been partially Romanized similarly upheld certain customs of shamanism. In Scotland, the native Picts and Gaels, as well as the Germanic-speaking Angles who came from Northumbria, maintained shamanistic traditions as well.

Stonehenge, a prehistoric monument located in Wiltshire, England.
https://unsplash.com/photos/Hl8LPagOrKs

Celtic Shamanism in Ireland

The Gaels who lived in Ireland before the arrival of the Vikings displayed many beliefs and customs associated with shamanism. The mythological tales formulated by the culture included a spiritual realm known as the "Otherworld," where their deities and the souls of the dead resided. The Otherworld figures appear in many myths and legends that developed during the earliest eras of Ireland. When the Vikings arrived in the 9th century, causing the people to become the Norse-Gaels, the similarities in traditional religious beliefs between the Gaelic and Norse cultures caused their mythology and customs to mesh fairly well.

Around the 12th century, Anglo-Norman invaders conquered portions of the country, while the later 16th and 17th-century colonization by England brought many English and people from the Scottish Lowlands to the northern regions. These new cultures' influence caused shamanism's evolution into a more homogenized form, and modern Celtic shamanism traces its ancestry back through the ages to all these different lineages. Because Ireland still maintains a strong Celtic character, many pockets of communities have brought Celtic shamanism into the 21st century.

Celtic Shamanism in England and Wales

The traditions of shamanism in England and Wales primarily stemmed from the Angles and Saxons, particularly after they transformed into the Anglo-Saxons. The Frisians and Jutes possessed some aspects of shamanism within their cultures. As they became absorbed by the Anglo-Saxon people following the incursion of the Romans into the British Isles, it developed a distinctly Celtic flavor. Once Christianity began to spread throughout Europe and arrived in England and Wales, the tug-of-war between the pagan and Christian religions eventually ended in favor of the latter.

Celtic Shamanism in Scotland

The Picts and Gaels who dwelt in ancient Scotland were both Celtic; therefore, they had shamanistic traditions like their brethren in Ireland. During the Roman conquest of the British Isles, the Romans never managed to gain much territory in Scotland, and the constant warfare between the natives and the invaders eventually resulted in the construction of Hadrian's Wall, built by the Roman emperor Hadrian, and the Antonine Wall erected by Hadrian's successor, Antoninus Pius. By the 5th century, the Romans had been mostly driven out of the British Isles, and the Saxons moved into Scotland.

Around the 6th century, Scotland was divided between the Picts, the Anglo-Saxons, and the Gaelic settlers from Ireland. Vikings later supplanted these cultures in the Northern Isles of Orkney and Shetland, and there was some Norse influence on the mainland afterward. This mix of Celtic, Anglo-Saxon, and Pictish cultures had Christian and pagan characteristics, while shamanism in the region took on aspects of both religions. The practitioners of shamanism in Scotland during the Middle Ages were sometimes regarded with suspicion. Still, their abilities to commune with the spiritual realm and their knowledge of herbalism and healing made them indispensable to their communities.

The Celts

Determining how to define who the Celts are can be tricky. Historically, there has been debate over whether to consider them an ethnicity, language, or culture. Currently, most modern scholars define Celts as "speakers of the Celtic languages" rather than any ethnocultural group. The primary historical Celtic peoples include the Britons, the Boii, the Celtiberians, the Gaels, the Gauls, the Gallaeci, the Galatians, and the Lepontii, as well as their offshoots. The six living Celtic languages are Breton, Irish, Scottish Gaelic, Welsh, Cornish, and Manx. The first four are considered continuous living languages, as they have been spoken by an unbroken line of cultures, while the latter two are revived languages, having once fallen out of use, but resurrected and reconstructed.

Extinct Dialects of the Celtic Language

There have been sixteen dialects of the Celtic language spoken throughout history, but ten of them have gone extinct. Most of the dead dialects were only spoken by people not native to the British Isles and had primarily developed in Continental Europe. The Celtic languages that have gone extinct include Celtiberian, Gallic, Noric, Galwegian Gaelic, Cumbric, Cisalpine Gaulish, Transalpine Gaulish, Pictish, Galatian, and Lepontic. Due to these languages evolving from foreign influences and the later Roman conquest of both Continental Europe and parts of the British Isles, they eventually disappeared and became considered extinct.

Shamans of the Celtic People

The shamans found among the ancient Celtic people had a certain mystical aura about them. There is little doubt that their contemporaries felt that they appeared peculiar to an extent. The use of entheogens, inducing a trance-like state in which they could commune with the spiritual realm, and their abilities to speak to both living and dead spirits set them apart from the rest of their society. Shamans were both loved and feared since they could seemingly discern secrets they shouldn't have been able to uncover without ever speaking to another living being. This gave them a position of prominence in their culture, but they remained separate from everyone else.

The Roles of Shamans

Most shamans of the Celtic people in the British Isles were considered revered elders and advisors, and in some cases, even leaders of their people. They possessed a mastery over spiritual and medicinal matters, making them akin to doctors and priests. Whenever a member of their tribe or village got sick or injured, the afflicted individuals would be sent to see their local shaman. Through a variety of means, the shaman would practice their craft to render aid and medical assistance to the ailing party. This included the application of medicinal herbs and poultices, as well as certain consumable concoctions to help ease the effects of certain illnesses and injuries.

If members of the community were in need of advice, they would often consult their shaman, who sought answers from the spirits. They were also responsible for determining which spirits were benevolent and which were malevolent, seeking only to cause chaos among the people. Trickster spirits were especially dangerous since they sometimes posed as benevolent ones, offering seemingly-innocuous advice that was actually meant to harm the individual in question. A good shaman could figure out when a spirit was trying to deceive them, warding them off through rituals and prayers.

Spirituality in Shamanism

Spirituality within shamanism refers to the search for meaning and a purpose in life in relation to the sanctity of the world. Part of a shaman's mandate is to assist the people of their community in finding their sacred meaning or purpose. This often resulted in the shaman serving as a guide as an individual undertook a vision quest, overseeing the person's spiritual journey as they confronted their inner mind and soul. Some of this guidance would come through interpreting the imagery and symbolism that a person saw while on their vision quest. It wasn't up to a shaman to tell the individual what their purpose might be, hey would merely help lead each person to the conclusions made on their own.

Magic in Shamanism

As it relates to shamanism, magic is very closely linked to the kind practiced by Wicca and Druidry. The purpose of their magic is to affect the living world through rituals, spells, prayers, and divination. It is a manipulation of the energy that dwells within all living things and the power of the soul. This can also be called an "aura," which is the potential energy emitted by humans, animals, flora, and the elements. Learning how to harness this potential energy and tap into it to use magic is one of the main goals of all shamans.

However, do not mistake shamanistic magic for the type of magic typically seen in works of fiction. They do not cast thunderbolts or throw fireballs around, and there is certainly no sparkling energy spewing out of magic wands. Real magic is subtler, working invisibly to cause a change in the potential energy that exists all around us. When using magic, it can be difficult for an external observer to actually identify what is occurring with it. Even the person affected by magic may not realize what has been done, chalking up their experiences to pure luck.

Shamanism and the Celtic Pagans

Unlike other religious practices, shamanism does not necessarily include a single supreme being or a pantheon of gods. Instead, the spirits of the dead, animals, and personifications of abstract concepts are the primary "higher powers" with which they commune. It can be seen as more of a supplemental religion typically practiced alongside more traditional religions, such as paganism or monotheistic deism. Shamans' main responsibility was to the people, whereas priests or Druids were beholden to the gods.

The Celtic paganism that arose in the British Isles before the Christianization of the area included a pantheon with various gods. The specific brand of shamanism practiced by the Celtic culture was influenced by this, such as a larger role played by the elements and nature, which can sometimes cause confusion between shamans and Druids. However, while Druids focused on nature itself, shamans were chiefly concerned with the spirits that exist as an extension of nature.

Chapter 3: Who Are the Druids?

Druids were among the highest-ranking members of ancient Celtic society. They were not merely religious leaders. They also served as keepers of lore, healers, adjudicators, legal authorities, and political advisors. There were many similarities between Druids and shamans in Celtic culture, but they had enough differences that the roles were not interchangeable. It was not uncommon for a community to have both Druids and shamans serving them.

Druids were among the highest-ranking members of ancient Celtic society.

History of the Druids

The first extensive references to the existence of Druids came from the *Bellum Gallicum* by Julius Caesar in 58-49 BCE. In it, he described the various roles of Druids living in Gaul, inhabited by both the Celtic and Aquitani tribes. Caesar wrote about their religious practices and societal hierarchy, including how most Druids remained in power for the duration of their lifetime. Interestingly, while a Druid leader's successor sometimes came to power through violence, more often than not, a new one was chosen through popular vote. While Caesar's scholarship focused on Druids in Continental Europe, it is likely to be very close to how Druidry worked in the British Isles.

In ancient Wales, Druids were some of the most important members of Celtic society. Although there are no written records concerning their earliest appearances, oral traditions usually date their presence in Wales to at least the 4th century BCE, but they may have been around much earlier. They were revered by the people they led, as they were viewed as the definitive link between humanity, nature, and the gods. Stonehenge, a prehistoric monument in Wiltshire, England, is believed to have been built sometime during the 30th or 29th century BCE. It is theorized to have been raised by the Druids as a sacred ceremonial site where they practiced important religious gatherings and rituals.

With the Roman conquest of the British Isles between 43-87 AD and the advent of Christianity, the Druids were pushed further and further toward the fringes of society. Christian priests and other church leaders were given prominence, diminishing the influence that Druids were able to exert. While Druidry survived in some form until the Middle Ages, it became effectively extinct not long after, being consigned to a few isolated pockets in England, Scotland, and Ireland, where practitioners struggled to preserve their religion amid an ever-increasing irrelevance. Some aspects of Christianity in the British Isles adopted Druid themes and symbols, syncretizing parts of Druidry with their own sacred figures and practices.

It wasn't until the 18th century that a renewed interest in Druidry resulted in its revival as a neopagan religion. One of the first neopagan Druidic organizations was founded in 1781 by Henry Hurle called the Ancient Order of Druids (AOD). The Druid Order is another major religious group that was founded by a man named George Watson MacGregor Reid in 1909. These religions sought to recreate as closely as possible their historical counterparts. However, one part of ancient Druidry not retained was the ritualistic sacrifices that many asserted they practiced, including sacrificing both sacred animals and human beings. This was due to the growing awareness of human and animal rights that started to take hold in the British Isles and society at large. In other areas, the Romanticism movement also tended to avoid the darker parts of the culture in favor of an overly generous depiction of the past. This is where the idea of the "noble savage" was first developed.

Roles of Druids

Druids were leaders and high-ranking members of their communities, being at the top of the three tiers with prominent warriors and serfs below them. However, this was not their only role in Celtic society. They often served a wide range of functions, making them indispensable to their people. In many instances, a Druidic leader was one of the few literate people in their community, placing the responsibility on them to carry out tasks that others were not equipped to handle. Their education and scholarship allowed them to gain insight into subjects that might otherwise elude their fellow tribespeople. This resulted in the Druid leaders bearing the burden of compiling their knowledge and wisdom into a form that could be passed down to future generations.

As keepers of lore, Druids were the authority on Celtic deities and history. They didn't maintain many written records but passed the lore on through oral traditions. Druids also used their depth of knowledge to serve their people by seeing to their medical needs. Being educated, they had experience with herbs and medical techniques to aid any sick or injured community members. While this aspect of Druidry has some overlap with shamanism, shamans typically focused on healing through spiritual means, while Druids sought to use their knowledge about nature to treat the physical symptoms.

Druids were often the final word on matters of law and justice. They were the arbiters of conflict and adjudicators who handed down a final judgment when people were accused of criminal acts. In this role, Druids had quite a bit of leeway regarding how they chose to punish those accused of breaking the law, with execution or exile being the harshest penalties one could incur. However, in most cases, a Druid would need to step in to render judgment due to conflicts over land, property, and interpersonal issues. Since there was no codified set of legal regulations for Druids, how they chose to handle each matter was entirely up to them.

While Druids usually held a leadership position within their community, they were not always the ultimate authority. In the instances where a secular leader held a higher station of power than them, they would serve as a political advisor, much the same as shamans. This became more common as society shifted from a religious focus to putting more emphasis on martial prowess. A warrior chieftain would have total control over their clan or tribe but would still consult with their Druids before making any politically significant decisions, especially regarding their interactions with rival groups.

Beliefs of Druids

Druidry has a core set of beliefs that remained consistent from its earliest days to the present time. It is these beliefs that both set it apart from and make it compatible with shamanism. The similarities between the two are significant enough that they are often confused. Still, it's a mistake to use the terms "Druid" and "shaman" interchangeably. Highlighting the common features as well as the differences can help to exemplify their relationship with each other.

Lack of Dogma

Somewhat paradoxically, one of Druidry's core beliefs is that they don't have a rigid belief system. As a religion, there is a stronger emphasis on personal experience than on pre-established tenets. Unlike Christianity, there are no strict commandments concerning how a practitioner behaves or the actions they can and cannot take. This lack of dogma makes Druidry much more of a loose affiliation of ideas and concepts than a belief system with firm boundaries.

Nature Worship

Nature is a major facet of Druidry, as many of their practices stem from believing in nature as a divine source. While some Druids are animists like shamans, they view nature's power as a construct in and of itself rather than possessing energy that manifests in the spiritual realm. There is a preoccupation with maintaining balance within nature, ensuring that a healthy life cycle can be perpetuated endlessly. This can be seen in how Druids will regard certain parts of nature as personifications of divine beings, such as worshiping certain deities, such as the god Dagda and goddess Daron through oak trees.

The Afterlife

The concept of an afterlife doesn't exist in Druidry in the same way in other religions, such as the Christian belief in Heaven, Hell, Purgatory, and Limbo. Instead, they maintain that those who die can return through reincarnation. The Druidic perspective is that those whose spiritual power is potent enough will return to the living world as a new being, either human, animal, or an important part of nature. They also believe that some people will transition from the world of the living to a peaceful, all-encompassing afterlife known as the Otherworld.

The Otherworld

The Otherworld in Druidry is similar to the shamanistic version with the same name. After a person has fulfilled their ultimate purpose in life, they are rewarded by passing on to the Otherworld, where they get the chance to dwell among mythological beings and deities. Suppose someone should decide that they would prefer to return to the living world. In that case, they may be given the opportunity to be reincarnated. However, the specific form that their new physical body takes is often left up to the whims of the higher powers.

Interconnectivity

Like shamanism, Druids have a belief in the interconnectivity of all life. However, where they differ is in the actual way this interconnection works. Shamans focus on the relationship between the physical world and the spiritual realm. In contrast, Druids view interconnectivity as the web of life between humans, animals, and the rest of nature. Plants, flowers, and trees provide oxygen, fruits, vegetables, and other resources, with smaller animals feeding on nuts and plants and larger animals consuming the smaller ones. Humans eat animals, grains, fruits, and vegetables while utilizing other natural resources, planting new seeds, or protecting crops while maintaining natural harmony.

Magic

Magic is a key component of Druidry, even more so than in other contemporary religions. Most of the magic that makes up the Druidic belief system is rooted in nature, with the goal being a balance between all living things. They use rituals, spells, prayers, relics, and divination to help them employ magic for the benefit of their people. To Druids, magic is another natural part of the world, and using it is no different than starting a fire to cook and keep warm or collecting water for washing and drinking.

They believe that nature is filled with magical energy that can be harnessed and redirected to aid in their endeavors.

Modern Druids

Modern Druids come from a neopagan tradition that has painstakingly recreated the ancient Druidic religion from all available sources, making it as authentic as possible. Most modern Druids are members of this religious movement, and while there are official organizations like the Druid Order and the AOD, not every Druid is required to be part of them. Some operate independently, looking to the forebears' example to guide their actions as leaders, healers, and protectors of nature.

The Ancient Order of Druids

The AOD is the oldest continuous Druidic order in the modern world. In a nod to the position within the society of their ancient ancestors, their motto is "Justice, Philanthropy, and Brotherly Love." They are active in the United Kingdom and France, operating branches across both counties. The AOD is run by the Imperial Grand Arch-Druid, and the person on whom that title is conferred is normally chosen through a vote by their regular members. The order attempts to assimilate their beliefs and actions into the modern world, volunteering within their communities and assisting with charitable endeavors. There is a strong emphasis on protecting nature, especially as environmental issues are rapidly becoming a hot topic throughout the Western world.

The Druid Order

The Druid Order propagates a philosophy of personal experience over academic learning, believing that any information gained from books or the classroom is not as useful as the wisdom acquired through actions in the real world. They also strongly focus on meditation as an overarching activity for all members. When the order holds meetings, they will discuss topics that range from philosophy, mythology, astrology, poetry, and history to debates on contemporary politics and religion. The highest authority within the Druid Order is a position known as the Chief Druid, who generally serves for whatever length of time they desire and normally chooses their successor personally.

Practices of Modern Druids

Because modern Druidry is both a revival and an extension of ancient Druidry, they share many of the same beliefs and practices. Other than ritual sacrifices, they maintain the traditions popular throughout the British Isles in the pre-Roman and pre-Christian eras. Keeping in mind that the world has changed quite a bit since that time, neopagan practitioners of Druidry have learned how to integrate their belief system into modern society, such as utilizing communication tools like the internet to connect with one another over long distances and across regional borders.

As the development of human civilization continues to extend into the untouched pockets of nature that have remained undisturbed, modern Druids serve as advocates for the environment. They seek to remind people of the beauty and power of the natural world and the benefits of keeping existing ecosystems intact. With many groups of animals becoming endangered and on their way to extinction, it is more important than ever for the Druidic philosophy to have a voice within modern cultures. If we're not careful enough to preserve nature, it could have dire consequences for future generations.

Druids vs. Shaman

For a quick overview of Druids versus shamans, you can refer to this chart below:

Druidry	Shamanism
Roles: Community leader; healer; political advisor; adjudicator; legal authority; lore keeper	Roles: Spiritual, political, and personal advisor; healer; seer; cultural leader
Afterlife: Reincarnation; the Otherworld	Afterlife: The spiritual realm (lower, middle, upper levels); the Otherworld
Interconnectivity: Humans, animals, and nature	Interconnectivity: The physical world and spiritual realm
Focus: Nature	Focus: Spirits
Magic: Spells; rituals; sacrifices; divination; prayers	Magic: Visions; vision quests; trances; rituals; prayers; divination; spells

Chapter 4: Celtic Deities and Symbols

Part of Celtic paganism is its unique mythology and symbols. As with many religions, these are important to the larger culture, providing tales of historically-significant figures intermingled with mythical heroes and gods and giving meaning through imagery and iconography. Celtic paganism doesn't have a strict "pantheon" like other religions, such as the Greek and Roman pagans or Norse and Egyptian mythology. Instead, it is more of a loose affiliation of deities that are culturally important and worshiped on an individual basis.

Part of Celtic paganism is its unique mythology and symbols.
Art Gongs, CC BY-SA 4.0 <https://creativecommons.org/licenses/by-sa/4.0>, via Wikimedia Commons: https://commons.wikimedia.org/wiki/File:Celtic_Tree_Of_Life_Art_Gong.jpg

Celtic Deities

There is a wide variety of Celtic deities due to the disparity between those worshiped regionally and those with a universal place within the religion. Many of these deities fall into categories based on specific characteristics, sharing these features with different deities that change from one locale to another. In Ireland, the primary gods are known as the Tuatha Dé Danann, who fought both the Fir Bolg and the Fomorians for dominion of the Otherworld. Welsh mythology sets its deities in the real world, but gods and supernatural beings exist alongside Arthurian heroes and villains. Here is a list of the different categories for the Celtic deities, as well as the most prominent ones within them:

Chief Gods

The chief gods are those who are considered either great leaders or important mythological figures. They include:

Lugh

A major warrior king and chief god who is usually depicted as part of the Tuatha Dé Danann. Lugh appears primarily in Irish mythology, although variants have shown up in other regions. The main features of Lugh include his weapon, known as the Spear of Assal, which was said to be impossible to overcome, and his mighty horse, Aenbharr, that could carry him at great speeds across both land and water. Lugh is involved in many tales within the Irish mythological cycle, and he lends his name to the pagan harvest festival of Lughnasadh.

Taranis

A god of thunder who is sometimes equated with Zeus or Jupiter and has been worshiped in Ireland, Britain, Hispania, and Gaul. Taranis is usually shown wielding a lightning bolt in one hand and a solar wheel in the other. Due to his position as a thunder god, he is considered a chief god in many regions that practiced Celtic paganism. However, his exact status is not always the same. In some locales, Taranis is above all other gods, while in other places, he is seen as one or two tiers below the local chief god.

Toutatis

Considered a protector of tribes, taking up his war hammer to smite the foes of those he is charged with safeguarding. Many Celtic tales place him alongside Lugh and Taranis as a trio of chief gods, and Toutatis has been equated to both Hermes/Mercury and Ares/Mars. As a skilled and dangerous warrior, he is typically said to be invincible in battle, and at other times, he is shown as a healer. Ancient Roman sources claimed that the Celtic pagans would make human sacrifices to Toutatis by casting people headfirst into a vat of an unknown liquid.

Esus

A god of the ancient Celtic Britons and Celtic pagans in Gaul, he was typically depicted as a large, axe-wielding warrior. One of the most famous images of Esus shows him hewing trees with his massive axe. Esus' name means passion, energy, and well-being, so he can be interpreted as a virile figure of battle and protection. In some traditions, he will aid those who invoke his name through a magical charm. Like Toutatis, Esus is associated with human sacrifice, and people were sacrificed to him during a ritual that included tying the victim to a tree and flogging them to death.

Mother Goddesses

The mother goddesses in Celtic paganism are known as "matronae," meaning "matrons." These goddesses tend to be closely identified with nature and the earth. The regional variants of the matronae include:

Modron, Rhiannon, and Dôn

These three are Welsh deities who represent different aspects of the mother goddess. Modron can be translated to "great mother," Rhiannon means "great queen," while Dôn is the mother of three important mythological figures who are known collectively as the "Children of Dôn." Modron is noted as the mother of Mabon ap Modron, who was said to be part of King Arthur's warband in the older Welsh version of Arthurian mythology. Some scholars have equated Modron with the later character of Morgan le Fay; thus, her son is seen as the precursor to Sir Mordred.

Rhiannon is a strong motherly figure who originated in the Otherworld and rules over a realm alongside her chosen consort, Pwyll Pen Annwn. She is often described as a giantess who is as strong as a horse, able to carry a dozen men upon her back. Some stories depict her as riding slowly across the Otherworld, always in view yet always out of reach. Because of her connection to horses, Rhiannon is sometimes compared to the Gaulish goddess Epona, who is usually shown in the form of a mare.

Dôn represents the power of motherhood through birthing and raising a trio of heroic figures. Her older son Gwydion fab Dôn is a trickster hero and magician. Her younger son Gilfaethwy is constantly living in his brother's shadow, and his deeds can be viewed as less heroic, although he suffers a magical form of punishment that is reminiscent of the twelve labors of Hercules. Her daughter Arianrhod is cursed by a mythical Welsh king and must outsmart him in order to break the three curses and gain her freedom.

Boand, Ernmas, Danu, and Macha

These are Irish deities who represent the mother goddess category in a similar manner to their Welsh counterparts. Boand is well known for giving birth to the god Aengus by having an affair with Dagda while her husband Elcmar is sent away on an errand. When he returns, Dagda hides Boand's pregnancy by causing the sun to stand still, preventing Elcmar from noticing the passage of time. Nine months later, Aengus is born, and Dagda restarts the sun. This has been proposed to be an ancient mythological origin for the dark, cold winter months.

Ernmas is notable for giving birth to three important trinities of children that feature heavily in the Irish variation of Celtic mythology. The eldest trio consists of Ériu, Fódla, and Banba, a trinity of war goddesses. The middle trio consists of the goddesses known as the Morrígan, named Anann, Badb, and Macha. The youngest trio consists of three sons: Coscar, Glonn, and Gnim. Unfortunately, despite the fame of her children, Ernmas was killed early on during the First Battle of Mag Tuired, when the Tuatha Dé Danann prevailed over the Fir Bolg.

Danu is considered the mother goddess of the Tuatha Dé Danann, an ancestor of the many deities in Irish mythology. Macha is an earth and sovereignty goddess heavily associated with the Irish province of Ulster. She is also a daughter of Ernmas and a member of the Morrígan, representing a warrior's glorious death in battle. She and her sisters are also seen as omens of doom and are related to the figure of the banshee in later Irish folklore.

Healing Deities

The healing deities in Celtic paganism come from numerous sources. They are often associated with herbalism, thermal springs, healing wells, and light. The healing deities include:

Brighid and Airmed

Brighid and Airmed are Irish goddesses known for their healing powers. Brighid is a member of the Tuatha Dé Danann, and she is a patron of not just healing but also wisdom, poetry, blacksmithing, protection, and domesticated animals. She is also related to the Celtic Briton goddess Brigantia, representing victory in war. Airmed participated in the Second Battle of Mag Tuired, healing anyone injured on the battlefield. After her father killed her brother, she wept at his grave for so long that her tears watered the earth, giving rise to all the healing herbs throughout the world.

Dian Cécht

A god of healing who was one of the Tuatha Dé Danann, fighting in the battles against both the Fir Bolgs and the Fomorians. Dian Cécht would heal the injured by submerging them in a healing well. When Nuada, the first king of the Tuatha Dé Danann, lost his arm during one of the wars against the Fomorians, Dian Cécht made him a new one out of silver, but it was able to function like a normal arm. However, when Dian Cécht's son, Miach, was able to fashion a flesh and blood arm to replace the silver one, Dian Cécht killed him out of jealousy. The tears of his daughter, Airmed, gave rise to all the healing herbs in the world, but after she collected them in one place, Dian Cécht again became jealous, scattering them across the four winds and preventing anyone from having complete knowledge of every healing herb in existence.

Belenus, Borvo, and Grannus

They are Celtic gods of healing who were worshiped in parts of Britain conquered by the Romans. Belenus is similar to the god Apollo and is closely associated with horses and chariots. Occasionally, he has been depicted as riding a horse-drawn chariot across the sky, carrying the sun with him like Apollo. Borvo is believed to offer healing through thermal springs, and it's said that he has infused the water with a special salve known only to him. Grannus is also related to thermal springs and mineral water, but it is more the soothing aspect of heat that is claimed to be his forte.

Water Deities

As one of the four elements, water is an incredibly important part of Celtic life. All living things require water to survive, and using it for cleansing purposes has given it an association with purity and virginity. Water gods and goddesses in Celtic paganism include:

Manannán, Lir, and Nodens

These three gods are water deities, but each one represents slightly different aspects of this element. Manannán is a great warrior and king who lived in the Otherworld, where he is a god of the sea. He has a boat called the Sguaba Tuinne, or Wave-Sweeper, that can propel itself across the water. Manannán also possesses the power to use mist from the ocean to make himself and his surroundings completely invisible to human eyes. Lir is the father of Manannán and the god of the oceans. He is a personification of the fury of the sea, exhibited by large waves crashing against the shore or tossing sailing vessels to and fro as if they were mere toys. Nodens is part healer and part warrior and is associated with the sea and hunting dogs.

Sulis, Damona, and Bormana

These goddesses are both water deities and healing deities, as they represent water's healing and purification properties. Sulis is a Celtic goddess worshiped in Britain, and she is a patron of the thermal spring near the city of Bath that is believed to encourage recovery and rejuvenation. While she is a life-giving and nourishing deity, her name is also invoked in several curses meant to strike down the foes of her venerators. Damona and Bormana both inhabit similar roles, being female counterparts to the god Borvo. They are associated with water and thermal springs like Borvo, with Damona linked to the hot spring at Bourbonne-les-Bains, and Bormana to the one in Saint-Vulbas.

Antlered Deities

The antlered deities in Celtic paganism typically represent hunters, the wilderness, and wild animals. Due to their association with a stag, the antlered deities are considered male, and part of their power comes from their masculinity. The antlered deities include:

Cernunnos

He is an Irish god who is usually shown sitting cross-legged and surrounded by bulls, stags, rams, horned serpents, and dogs. Cernunnos is a figure of great power and can be seen as a counterpart to the mother goddesses. As with other antlered gods, he symbolizes male potency and the untamed wilderness. Some stories depict Cernunnos as a heroic figure, aiding demigods such as Fráech when he attempts to rescue his wife and son from evil beings who kidnapped them during a cattle raid.

Brân the Blessed

A Welsh god, sometimes depicted as a horned giant, is a mythical high king. Brân is known to be a skilled hunter, often riding his massive steed both into battle and on the trail of dangerous prey. His name is translated as "crow" or "raven." As an interesting aside, author George R. R. Martin has used the name "Bran" for a character in his book series "A Song of Ice and Fire," later adapted into the television series "Game of Thrones." In the narrative, Bran is closely associated with a being known as the Three-Eyed Crow or Bloodraven.

Other Deities

Many other deities are connected to Celtic paganism. The concepts they represent vary wildly, including hammers, eloquence, horses, divine bulls, and the sun. The deities belonging to these different categories include:

Sun Goddesses: Áine and Olwen

Áine and Olwen are both considered sun goddesses, although scholars have sometimes questioned their status as solar deities. In Irish mythology, Áine is associated with the midsummer sun, possessing the qualities of sovereignty and wealth. Because she represents the summer, she is occasionally depicted as a red mare with a fiery mane and hooves. Olwen is said to be as beautiful as the burning sun, wearing a red dress engulfed in flames, having bright yellow hair that looks like fire, and adorned with many golden rings.

God of Hammers: Sucellos

A Celtic god who is always shown holding an enormous hammer or mallet. Despite this, he is typically worshiped as a god of agriculture, wine, and beer. The reason he is always carrying a hammer or mallet is unknown, but several tales call him a "good striker," implying that he can use his weapon in battle when necessary. In addition, Sucellos protects the fields and forests and serves as a guardian of boundaries. He has also been equated with Silvanus, the Roman god of the forests. Both are known to have protected flocks of sheep from hungry wolves, skinning and wearing the pelts of those they have slain.

Gods of Eloquence and Strength: Ogmios and Oghma

Ogmios is a Celtic god of eloquence and strength, using his persuasive abilities to bind men to his causes. However, he is also noted for his superhuman strength and able to perform incredible feats of physical prowess. He can be seen as an analog to both Heracles and Odysseus from Greek mythology. Oghma is a similar god from Irish mythology, serving as the champion of Nuada, king of the Tuatha Dé Danann. He is credited as the creator of Ogham, the Celtic tree alphabet.

Horse Deities: Epona and Atepomarus

Epona is a horse goddess in Celtic mythology, originally worshiped by the people of Gaul and later migrating to the British Isles. She is a goddess of fertility and a protector of horses, ponies, mules, and donkeys. In some traditions, she serves as a psychopomp, leading her steeds as they carry souls into the afterlife. Atepomarus, also associated with horses, is also a healer. His name can translate to "great horseman," and when venerated by the Celts, they would leave small horse figurines around his shrines.

The Divine Bull: Tarvos Trigaranus

He is a Celtic god who takes on the form of a large bull and is associated with Esus. In artwork depicting both Tarvos Trigaranus and Esus, the former usually looms over the latter but is somewhat hidden behind or within a tree that Esus is chopping down. As the Divine Bull, Tarvos Trigaranus represents power, potency, stamina, hard work, determination, confidence, and wealth. The ancient Celtic pagans would sometimes sacrifice a bull during religious ceremonies, as an offering of such magnitude was often taken as a sign of great respect.

Celtic Symbols

Many symbols, images, and iconography are considered sacred to the Celtic people. Each of these represents aspects of Celtic society that are deemed important or relevant to their daily lives. Some symbols possess religious connotations, while others are more defined by cultural traits. The following list includes the Celtic symbols that are most often associated with their people:

The Celtic Cross: ☦

The Celtic Cross is a variation on the Latin cross, appearing like a lowercase "t" with a circle around the intersection of the two limbs. This is sometimes interpreted as a halo. It originated in Ireland during the Middle

Ages, around the time when Christianity began to spread across the British Isles, pushing the Celtic pagans to the fringes of society. To avoid being completely usurped, the Celtic people adopted some of the imagery from Christianity, incorporating it into their own iconography. There are different interpretations of what the Celtic Cross signifies. Some believe the four limbs represent the four Cardinal directions (north, south, east, and west). In contrast, others claim it symbolizes the four seasons (spring, summer, autumn, and winter) or the four stages of the day (morning, midday, evening, and midnight).

The Celtic Tree of Life:

The Celtic Tree of Life is called "Crann Bethadh" in Irish. It is usually depicted as a large tree with interwoven roots and branches. It is a symbol often associated with Druids. The Tree of Life represents harmony and balance, as its branches hold up the sky and its roots anchor the earth. This symbol is often created symmetrically so that it appears the same upside down and right side up. Since many Celtic cultures believed that spirits were dwelling within the trees, sometimes even the spirits of their ancestors, the Tree of Life provided a link between this world and the next.

The Triquetra:

The Triquetra is also known as the Celtic Triangle or the Trinity Knot. It has a continuous three-pointed symbol reminiscent of the shape of a leaf interwoven with a circle. The Triquetra represents unity, family, and eternal love, displaying the interlocking shapes as members of a family unit. Scholars believe it to be one of the oldest spiritual symbols associated with the Celtic people, originating in the Book of Kells, an illuminated manuscript written in the 9th century that contains the four Gospels of the New Testament, in addition to several other assorted texts and tables. The book was transcribed in Latin, but it contains various images from contemporary Ireland, Scotland, or England, including the Triquetra.

The Triskelion:

The Triskelion contains a triple spiral that represents the unity of the elements of fire, water, and earth. The name "Triskelion" stems from the Greek word "triskele," which means "three-legged." It was found in Neolithic and Bronze Age artifacts and Celtic depictions dating back from the Iron Age. Three is an important number in Celtic paganism. The Triskelion displays this with its three spiral patterns that swirl out from the center. It symbolizes progress and moving forward as an individual and a society. When the spirals are shown clockwise, it embodies a balance or harmony with nature. However, if the spirals are counter-clockwise, it is believed to assert an attempt to manipulate the natural order.

The Wicker Man:

The Wicker Man is a symbol from Celtic paganism that depicts an effigy of a large human made out of wicker, straw, and hay. The ancient Celtic people purportedly used it as a means for human or animal sacrifice. The victim would be secured within the Wicker Man, and then it would be set on fire as part of a pagan ceremony. Although there is little historical evidence to corroborate the accounts from ancient Greek and Roman sources, the Wicker Man as a symbol has endured through the years, becoming intrinsically linked with the Celtic pagans. Neopagan religions have adopted the Wicker Man in their rituals, albeit without human or animal sacrifices. They will often burn a wicker effigy as part of their Midsummer celebrations.

The Dara Celtic Knot:

The Dara Celtic Knot is an interwoven design resembling a series of crisscrossing knots in a somewhat grid-like pattern. Its name is derived from the Irish word for "oak tree," which is "doire." The symbol represents an ancient oak tree's root system, and it has no beginning or end, signifying the continuous cycles of life. The Celtic people and Druids strongly favor nature and consider oak trees sacred. It is also a symbol of strength, as the root system runs deep, allowing the tree to withstand the fury of the elements. The Dara Celtic Knot can be used for decoration. Still, it's also employed in spiritual charms and rituals performed by Druids and shamans.

The Claddagh Ring: 

The Claddagh Ring is a traditional Irish ring that contains the shape of a heart and a crown clasped together. The heart is meant to represent love, and the crown represents loyalty. Having the heart clasping the crown signifies friendship. They were first produced in Galway, Ireland, during the 18th century. Still, their popularity really began to boom in the Victorian age. The use of the Claddagh Ring spread beyond the British Isles during the late 19th and 20th centuries. How the ring is worn denotes different meanings. The heart pointing toward your wrist and worn on the left hand shows that you are married, and the heart pointing to your wrist on the right hand shows that you are in a relationship. The heart pointed out on the left hand shows that you are engaged, and the heart pointed out on the right hand shows you are single.

The Ailm:

The Ailm is derived from the letter of Ogham, or the Celtic tree alphabet, which shares its name. It is traditionally believed to depict a silver fir or conifer tree. It symbolizes inner strength, resilience, endurance, purification, good health, healing, and fertility. Being a symbol from a written form of communication, the Ailm carries the connotation of wisdom and knowledge, especially that which endures from generation to generation. The Celtic people greatly revered trees, so any imagery that represents them also embodies the characteristics associated with sacred trees.

The Wheel of Taranis:

The Wheel of Taranis is a symbol associated with the thunder god Taranis, as it is one of the two items he is depicted as holding in his hands, the other being a lightning bolt. It is shown as a circle with eight spokes extending from the center, giving it the appearance of a ship's helm. It represents the eight Gaelic festivals celebrated throughout the year by Celtic pagans and neopagans (Yule, Imbolc, Ostara, Beltane, Litha, Lughnasadh, Mabon, and Samhain). The Wheel of Taranis is emblematic of the cyclical nature of the world and how it continues turning in an endless loop of birth, maturity, death, and rebirth.

The Shamrock:

The Shamrock is an Irish staple, representing good fortune and luck. Druids use it as a symbol of the triad, as it is made up of three heart-shaped leaves. The importance of the number three can be seen in much of the Celtic and Druidic iconography since there is a belief that three is a sacred number. This can also be seen in Christian imagery, as the Holy Trinity also contains three beings - the Father, the Son, and the Holy Spirit. Shamrocks are considered the national plant of Ireland, where they can be found all across the land since they thrive in cool, damp climates.

The Celtic Motherhood Knot:

The Celtic Motherhood Knot represents the strong bond between a mother and her child. Although they can have a variety of designs, most include two hearts and triquetra intertwined with each other, signifying the familial relationship and love for one another. One heart is set lower than the other, denoting the generational aspect of the mother and child. The endless love symbolized by the Celtic Motherhood Knot has also been used by Celtic pagans with Christianity influences to represent the Madonna and her son, Jesus.

The Serch Bythol:

The Serch Bythol is a symbol created by two connected triquetras. Usually, one is a slightly different shade or color from the other, denoting two separate souls joining together in a union. It represents a deep, everlasting love, a powerful reminder of the strong emotions tied to a relationship. This symbol is typically chosen to denote an engagement or marriage, but it can be used for any serious partnership. The symmetrical halves demonstrate the unification of two minds, bodies, and spirits, while the circle in the middle shows the eternal love that binds them all together.

Chapter 5: Ogham: The Celtic Tree Alphabet

Ogham (pronounced "oh-uhm") is an alphabet used by the Celtic people thousands of years ago. It is also known as the Celtic tree alphabet because each of the letters correlates to a different type of tree. The simplicity of Ogham belies its functional complexity, as most of the letters consist of basic tally marks, dashes, and a few modest shapes. However, with a few exceptions, it can usually be transposed onto the Latin alphabet like a cipher since they share many similarities.

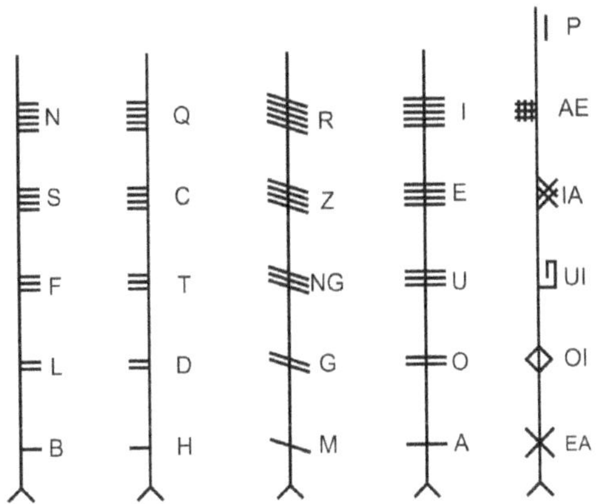

Ogham is an alphabet used by the Celtic people thousands of years ago.

Origins of Ogham

Ogham was developed between the 1st century BCE and the 4th century AD. It was used to record the first written sources of the Archaic Irish language, including over 400 orthodox inscriptions etched upon stone monuments scattered around Ireland and western Britain. Ancient Druids created these monuments from the 4th to the 6th century, as they were most likely the only literate members of Celtic society at that time. Later, from the 6th to the 9th centuries, Ogham evolved into writing Old Irish or Old Gaelic.

Since any examples of Ogham written on wood or other perishable materials have decomposed long ago, only those inscribed on stone survive. Many of these stones are actually grave markers, and a handful contains personal names and indicators of land ownership. In Ireland, Wales, Scotland, the Isle of Man, and southwest England, the stone monuments with Ogham inscriptions have been definitively identified as territorial signs and memorials to the dead. The only one of these stones that has a name of an individual with a historical record is the memorial to Vortiporius, a Welsh king who ruled Dyfed in the 6th century.

Legendary Account of Ogham's Origins

Medieval Irish folklore credits the creation of Ogham to a mythical Scythian king named Fenius Farsa. It claims that the alphabet came about at the same time as the Gaelic language, following shortly after the destruction of the Tower of Babel in the land of Shinar when the ability to understand the universal language was stripped from humanity. Fenius trekked from his home in Scythia to the ruins of the Tower of Babel alongside Íar mac Nema, Goídel mac Ethéoir, and a group of 72 scholars. They had hoped to study the confused languages left in the wake of the tower's fall, but upon their arrival, they discovered that these languages had already been scattered across the world.

Fenius charged his scholars with going out to find and study the dispersed languages while he remained at the tower and coordinated their efforts. Ten years later, the scholars returned, having completed their assignments, and Fenius took the best parts of each confused language, establishing the "selected language." He called his new language "Goidelic" in honor of Goídel mac Ethéoir. Later, he developed an extension of Goidelic known as "Íarmberla," named for Íar mac Nema, as well as

"Bérla Féne," which was named after himself. Finally, he perfected his language's writing system, dubbing it "Beithe-luis-nuin," otherwise known as "Ogham." Supposedly, the names of the letters in Ogham are that of his 25 best scholars.

Another legend ascribes the creation of Ogham to the god Oghma. He was said to be a skilled speaker and poet, having the ability to be very persuasive. His reasoning for developing this alphabet was to exclude any fools or rustic people, only wanting to associate with learned individuals. The first message written by Oghma in his new system was a series of seven b's on a piece of wood from a birch. This was meant to be a warning to his fellow god, Lugh, cautioning him that his wife would be stolen away seven times to the Otherworld unless he protected her with the birch. For this reason, the letter b in Ogham was named for the birch, and tradition holds that the other letters were given names after trees as well.

Purpose of Ogham

Two main theories have been proposed about why the Ogham was created. Scholars are split as to which theory they believe is correct, and there hasn't been a general consensus in favor of one over the other. Until more relics or artifacts containing Ogham are found, it's impossible to determine for certain which theory carries more weight. At this time, both have their merits, but they also have their detractors, as modern academia cannot account for all the missing information that would sway the minds of those who study Ogham.

Theory #1

The first theory is that the language was invented to serve as a cryptic alphabet, preventing anyone who is only familiar with the Latin alphabet from being able to decipher this writing. Ancient Druids could have used Ogham as a secret method of communication between Celtic tribes. They would have been able to talk about politics, military operations, intelligence gathering, and religion without fear of being exposed if their correspondences were intercepted. This was a particularly dangerous time for the Celtic people living in the British Isles, as they had to ensure the Romans occupying Britain did not discover their communications. There was a serious fear in Ireland that the Romans might invade their home next, and they wanted to be ready for any potential conflict in the future.

Centuries later, when the people of Ireland had launched their own invasion of western Britain, it would have continued to be useful for them to maintain the secrecy of their communications from the Romans or Romano-Britons that remained in the region. This is where the theory runs into some trouble. By this point, there were inscriptions in Wales that used Ogham and Latin together. Literacy had increased enough in the post-Roman British Isles that it would have been easy enough for any messages coded in Ogham to be deciphered, making it difficult to keep any plans from reaching their enemies.

Theory #2

The second theory is that Ogham was developed by the earliest Christian communities that arose in Ireland to have a unique alphabet when composing short inscriptions or messages in the Irish language. Archaic Irish included vocalized sounds that would have been difficult to transcribe using the Latin alphabet, necessitating the creation of a separate system. There was known to be a community of Christians living in Ireland in about 400 AD, whose existence was documented by Prosper of Aquitaine in the Universal Chronicle. Writing in 431 AD, prosper recounted the mission of Palladius, Bishop of Ireland, who was sent there by Pope Celestine I.

In the 4th century, Irish settlements appeared in the western parts of Wales. It is believed that a variation of Ogham was established here after the settlers intermingled with the Romano-Britons, who were well-versed in the Latin alphabet. This would explain the stone monuments found in Wales that contain both Ogham and Latin inscriptions. While it makes sense that these stones may have been the result of contact between Irish Christians and Romanized Britons, there is a lack of direct evidence concerning the creators of the Welsh stone monuments to prove this theory true.

Debunked Theory

There was originally a third theory that had previously been a part of Ogham scholarship, but it fell out of favor as studies of the language evolved to include more comprehensive examinations of the relationship between the culture and writings. This theory proposed that Druids living in Cisalpine Gaul around 600 BCE had concocted a secret system of hand and finger signals inspired by a variation of the Greek alphabet contemporaneous to Northern Italy. These hand signals were later transcribed through oral accounts or on wooden materials, making their way with the ancient Celts when they arrived in the British Isles. Eventually, this system was inscribed on the stone monuments during the days of the early Christians in Ireland.

This theory was debunked because later detailed studies proved Ogham was developed specifically for Archaic Irish during the earliest centuries AD. Any connection to the Greek alphabet has also been disproved, with there being only superficial commonalities between the two writing systems that do not hold up to deeper scrutiny. Modern scholars have almost unanimously rejected the theory as a viable interpretation of the origins of Ogham. The only part of the theory that has any relevance is the idea that the hand or finger signals were reflected through the use of tally marks to form the Ogham script.

Composition of Ogham

The individual letters that make up Ogham consist of 25 characters. They are based on tally marks, dashes, and basic symbols. Each character is assigned a corresponding value in the Latin alphabet, usually derived from the name of the Ogham letter in Archaic or Old Irish. Originally, there were only 20 characters, but 5 more were added over the centuries, bringing the total to 25. It is believed that the Ogham script was inspired by a counting system that predates the Celtic tree alphabet, based around the numbers 5 and 20. This system was then adapted by the first Oghamists.

Letters of Ogham

b—Beith (Old Irish: Beithe): Beith translates to "birch," which is also the tree associated with it in the arboreal tradition.

l—Luis (Old Irish: Luis): Luis translates to either "herb" or "flame." In the arboreal tradition, it is associated with "mountain-ash," also known as rowan.

w—Fearn (Old Irish: Fern): Fearn translates to "alder-tree," which is why it is associated with alder in the arboreal tradition. In Archaic Irish, it was spelled "wernā," which is why it has been ascribed the letter "w."

s—Sail (Old Irish: Sail): Sail translates to "willow," which is also the tree associated with it in the arboreal tradition.

n—Nion (Old Irish: Nin): Nion translates to "forked branch" or "loftiness." In the arboreal tradition, it is associated with ash.

j—Uath (Old Irish: Úath): Uath translates to "fear" or "horror." In the arboreal tradition, it is associated with "white-thorn," also known as hawthorn. The reason it has been ascribed the letter "j" is unclear as its original etymology is not known.

d—Dair (Old Irish: Dair): Dair translates to "oak," which is also the tree associated with it in the arboreal tradition.

t—Tinne (Old Irish: Tinne): Tinne translates to "iron bar" or "ingot." In the arboreal tradition, it is associated with holly.

k—Coll (Old Irish: Coll): Coll translates to "fair-wood" or "hazel-tree," which is why it is associated with hazel in the arboreal tradition.

kw—Ceirt (Old Irish: Cert): Ceirt translates to "fair" or "just." In the arboreal tradition, it is associated with apple trees.

m—Muin (Old Irish: Muin): Muin translates to "neck," "trick," or "esteem." In the arboreal tradition, it is associated with thickets of thorns. It is often mistakenly assigned an association with grape vines, but as grapes have never been successfully cultivated or grown in Ireland, this is an erroneous attribution.

g—Gort (Old Irish: Gort): Gort translates to "field" or "garden." In the arboreal tradition, it is associated with ivy.

gw—nGéadal (Old Irish: Gétal): nGéadal translates to the verbs "to wound" or "to stab." In the arboreal tradition, it is associated with a fern or broom. This letter's original phonetic value in Archaic Irish was "gw," the voiced labiovelar. This phoneme was merged with "g" (gort) in Old Irish, and medieval manuscripts assigned it the Latin letter "ng" (ŋ), which is why "nGéadal" is spelled with the initial "n-."

st—Straif (Old Irish: Straiph): Straif translates to "sulfur." In the arboreal tradition, it is associated with blackthorn.

r—Ruis (Old Irish: Ruis): Ruis translates to "red" or "reddening." In the arboreal tradition, it is associated with elderberries due to the practice of using the juice extracted from the berries to redden the cheeks.

a—Ailm (Old Irish: Ailm): Ailm's original translation cannot be definitely established, but some etymologists believe it is meant to represent a groan. In the arboreal tradition, it is associated with silver fir and conifer trees, or possibly pine trees.

o—Onn (Old Irish: Onn) Onn translates to "ash-tree," which is why it is associated with ash in the arboreal tradition.

u—Úr (Old Irish: Úr): Úr translates to "earth," "soil," "clay," "moist," and "fresh." In the arboreal tradition, it is associated with heather.

e—**Eadhadh (Old Irish: Edad):** Eadhadh has no known translation, but in the arboreal tradition, it is associated with "true-tree" or aspen.

i—**Iodhadh (Old Irish: Idad):** Iodhadh is sometimes translated as "yew," which is also the tree associated with it in the arboreal tradition.

The following letters are known as the "forfeda," which are additional letters added to the basic 20 signs of Ogham:

ea—**Éabhadh (Old Irish: Ébhadh):** Éabhadh has no known translation, but in the arboreal tradition, it is associated with aspen. It is also sometimes paired with Eadhadh, which is associated with the same tree.

oi—**Ór (Old Irish: Óir):** Ór translates to "gold." In the arboreal tradition, it is associated with "spindle-tree" or ivy.

ui—**Uilleann (Old Irish: Uilleand):** Uilleann translates to "elbow." In the arboreal tradition, it is associated with honeysuckle.

p/io—**Pín/Peithe/Ifín (Old Irish: Pín/Peithe/Iphín):** The letter Pín was added to Ogham several centuries after its creation since Archaic Irish did not have a "p." Later on, certain scholars believed the forfeda were all vowels, they added the letter Peithe, reassigning "p" from Pín to Peithe, which was pronounced with a soft "p," or "ph-" sound. The letter Ifín was given the value of "io" to account for this change. In the arboreal tradition, it is associated with gooseberries or thorns.

x/ai—**Eamhancholl (Old Irish: Emancholl):** Eamhancholl translates to "twins of coll" or "twins of hazel." Like the letter coll, it is associated with hazel in the arboreal tradition.

Chart of Ogham Characters

Beith (*b*)	Luis (*l*)	Fearn (*w*)	Sail (*s*)	Nion (*n*)
Uath (*j*)	Dair (*d*)	Tinne (*t*)	Coll (*k*)	Ceirt (*kʷ*)
Muin (*m*)	Gort (*g*)	nGéadal (*gʷ*)	Straif (*st*)	Ruis (*r*)

Ailm (*a*)	Onn (*o*)	Úr (*u*)	Eadhadh (*e*)	Iodhadh (*i*)
Éabhadh (*ea*)	Ór (*oi*)	Uilleann (*ui*)	Peithe/Ifín (*p/io*)	Eamhanchol l (*x/ai*)

Ogham Ciphers

When writing with Ogham, you can indicate the start and end of a sentence or phrase through the use of feather marks that look like this:)
⟨

The Ogham characters go in between, all running along a single horizontal line (Ogham can be written vertically as well, but it's much easier for those familiar with any languages that are written and read from left to right to use the horizontal configuration), leaving spaces between them to indicate the separation of words. For example, if you wanted to write "This is a cipher," here's how it would look in Ogham:

The phrase opens with a feather mark and then uses the characters Tinne (t), Uath (j), Iodhadh (i), Sail (s); Iodhadh (i), Sail (s); Ailm (a); Coll (k), Iodhadh (i), Peithe (p), Uath (j), Eadhadh (e), Ruis (r). It then ends with another feather mark. Note that the translation from English to Ogham is not a perfect 1:1, since they do not have all the same letters. The Uath's "j" is substituted for "h," and the Coll's "k" replaces the "c." In the former's instance, despite being written with a "j," Uath usually functions as an "h," and the latter case uses a "k" for the "c" because the letter "c" is only pronounced as a hard "c," or a "k" sound, rather than varying between a hard and soft "c" like in English.

To create an Ogham cipher by translating English to Ogham and vice versa, some letters from Ogham will be reused for more than one letter in English, while some are not used except under specific conditions. You can refer to the chart below for the basic translations from Ogham to the

Latin alphabet:

a	B	c/k	d
e	f/w*	g	h/j**
i	j/i***	k	l
m	N	o	p
q/k^w	R	s	t
u	v/w****	w	x
y/g^w	z/st		

*Since there is no equivalent for the Latin letter "f," it uses Fearn, as the "w" of Fearn is normally pronounced like a Latin "v."

**While Uath is represented by the letter "j," it is normally pronounced as if it was a Latin letter "h."

***Even though Uath is represented by the letter "j," it is not the equivalent of "j" in the Latin alphabet. Instead, the Latin Letter "j" uses Iodhadh, the same as the letter "i."

****There is no difference between the Latin "v" and "w" in Ogham, so both use the "w" of Fearn.

⫻

⫻

Ogham Cipher Exercises

See if you can decipher the following sentences encoded using Ogham:

Decoded: _ .

Decoded: _ .

Decoded: _ .

Answers:

1. "By the power of Grayskull, I have the power." [b(y/gʷ) t(h/j)e power o(f/w) gra(y/gʷ)skull i (h/j)a(v/w)e the power]
2. "With great power comes great responsibility." [wit(h/j) great power (c/k)omes great responsibilit(y/gʷ)]
3. "The only thing we have to fear is fear itself." [t(h/j)e onl(y/gʷ) t(h/j)ing we (h/j)a(v/w)e to (f/w)ear is (f/w)ear itsel(f/w)]

Chapter 6: Druidic Tree Astrology

Druidic Tree Astrology, also known as Celtic Tree Astrology, is a divinatory practice based on the beliefs of the ancient Druids. They maintained that the date and time a person was born was a significant aspect of how their personality formed. Because of this, the Druids made predictions as to what types of characteristics a person would develop as they matured into an adult.

Trees of Celtic Astrology

Birch

Birch Tree.

Title: The Achiever

Birthdates: December 24 to January 20

Traits: Loving, Ambitious, Courageous

Compatibility: Willow and Vine

You are a highly driven individual, possessing the capability to motivate other people. When a crisis arises, you will step forward to take charge of the situation, but you make sure to do it while keeping in mind the feelings and emotions of others. Because of your ambitious and determined nature, you seek ways to acquire knowledge and learn as much as possible. Your resilience in the face of adversity is evident, and despite your versatility, you are always striving for more. You can be quick-witted and charming, making friends easily and able to put a smile on people's faces.

Exercise to Try: Red Crane Focus Meditation

The red crane focus meditation technique is a great way to find balance in your life. Like the red crane that balances itself on one leg, you will be able to equally distribute your responsibilities and desires so that one doesn't outweigh the other. Keeping your life in harmony is important to remain happy and healthy. There are many things that meditation can help you with, including easing tension and ridding yourself of stress. This technique will grant you the serenity you deserve so that you can focus on the important things in life.

How to Do It:

1. Start by finding a place to sit. Make sure that you're comfortable. You can sit cross-legged or place the soles of your feet together, letting your knees fall to the side.

2. Close your eyes and begin to count while breathing. Inhale through your nose, counting to 4 as you fill your lungs with air.

3. Hold your breath while counting to 7. Visualize all your problems and stress being gathered into one place as if you were balling up a wad of paper.

4. Exhale through your mouth while counting to 8. Your breath out should be audible, making a whooshing sound. Picture that ball of problems and stress being blown out of your both, expelling it all from your body.

5. Repeat the 4-7-8 breathing technique 5 times, cleansing your body of any negative energy.

6. Relax the muscles in your jaw and face. Drop your shoulders and allow your hands and arms to go limp. Feel the muscles in your legs and feet relax as well. You should be completely at ease once you are through.

7. Visualize everything you need to take care of for the day, and then think about something you want to do for fun. Imagine them sitting on opposite sides of a scale. As you focus on balancing the scale, remind yourself that once you have fulfilled your responsibilities, you will allow yourself time to do something you enjoy.

8. Return your focus to your breathing and repeat the 4-7-8 technique for 5 more repetitions. On your final exhale, open your eyes. You should now have a clearer picture of how to go about your day while balancing your duties with your desires.

Rowan

Rowan Tree.
https://pixabay.com/es/photos/serbal-bayas-sorbus-planta-%c3%a1rbol-3571546/

Title: The Thinker

Birthdates: January 21 to February 17

Traits: Intelligent, Patient, Influential

Compatibility: Hawthorn and Ivy

You are the kind of person who has a clear vision of what you want, and you tend to set lofty goals for yourself. While appearing calm on the outside, there is a constant rush of energy on the inside that helps to inspire you. You have a great imagination and unique ideas, which can sometimes intimidate others. Your fierce nature and hardened exterior hide a patient, kind, and caring heart. Your capacity to improve your circumstances and those around you through a sharp, compassionate mind often prove a great boon to other people. While you may appear reserved, your silent determination draws people toward you.

Exercise to Try: Whispered Stillness Guided ASMR Meditation

Everyone who meditates has the goal of finding stillness during their exercises. Using a whispered stillness-guided ASMR meditation can lead you down that path, guiding you the whole way as your body and mind achieve the stillness you desire. ASMR can offer a soothing retreat from the chaos of the world around you, and hearing the sleep-inducing whispers from a calming voice can offer you a deep sense of serenity. The stillness will slowly wash over you until every part of you is completely relaxed, aiding you in drifting off to a restive and restorative sleep.

How to Do It:

Find a whispered stillness-guided ASMR meditation track on an audio website or app like Spotify, or use a video from YouTube. Allow the guided meditation to play from your smartphone or another electronic device, and close your eyes, following the instructions as you are guided to sleep.

Ash

Ash Tree.
https://pixabay.com/es/photos/fraxinus-excelsior-ceniza-844653/

Title: The Enchanter

Birthdates: February 18 to March 17

Traits: Artistic, Imaginative, Open-Minded, Independent

Compatibility: Reed and Willow

You have a fantastic personality that many people find enticing, but your shy nature means you prefer to spend plenty of time alone. The beauty of nature inspires you, and your creativity is seemingly boundless. The subjects that most interest you include art, science, writing, poetry, and spirituality. While others might view you as a bit of a recluse, you don't mind, as you have no problem immersing yourself in your own inner world of wonder and imagination. You constantly reinvent yourself and strive to do whatever makes you happy, regardless of what other people might think. Because of your creativity and independence, you inspire those around you to seek their own happiness.

Exercise to Try: Relaxing Early Morning Ocean Breath Meditation

You can tap into the calming power of ocean breath meditation early in the morning to aid you in getting your day started on the right foot. Relaxation will flow through you, washing away the tension and frustration that you might face at home, work, school, or just out in the world. Beginning the day with ocean breath meditation can stick with you all the way into the evening, keeping you centered and balanced for any curveballs life might throw at you.

How to Do It:

1. Sit up tall, close your eyes, and allow your shoulders to relax away from your ears. In preparation for this meditation, focus on your breathing without trying to control it. Start to inhale and exhale through your mouth instead of your nose.

2. Move your focus to your throat. When you exhale, try to tone the back of your throat (your glottis or soft palate). The goal is to slightly constrict the air passage. If you're having trouble with this, think of the way you fog up a pane of glass. There should be a soft hissing or wheezing sound.

3. When you are comfortable with this type of exhale, apply the same throat contraction to your inhalation. You should hear the same soft hissing or wheezing sound as you breathe. The name of this breathing technique is derived from that sound, as it resembles the sounds of the ocean. If you are a fan of "Star Wars," you might call

it Darth Vader Meditation since it also sounds like his iconic breathing.

4. Once you have full control of your throat while inhaling and exhaling, close your mouth and start breathing through your nose. Continue to apply the same toning to your throat as you did when you were breathing through your mouth. Your breaths will continue to make a similar noise as it moves in and out through your nose.

5. Breathe like this for about five minutes, using each exhale to push any intrusive thoughts out of your mind. This is a time to allow total relaxation to wash over your body, so you must empty your mind. It may help to focus your attention on your breathing, imagining that you are sitting on a beach near the seashore, listening to the ocean as it ebbs and flows.

Alder

Alder Tree.
https://pixabay.com/es/photos/del-aliso-negro-blackle-4681232/

Title: The Trailblazer

Birthdates: March 18 to April 14

Traits: Brave, Romantic, Generous

Compatibility: Birch and Oak

You are always on the move, and you dislike wasting time on superficiality. Positive energy about you is constantly projected out, drawing people toward you. You are also a natural leader, falling comfortably into the role even when you don't intend to take charge. There is an easy-going charm about you, and as an extrovert, you never have trouble mingling with a crowd, no matter what types of personalities are present. Your knack for getting along with everyone means people enjoy being in your company. There is an attractiveness to your self-confidence, making you seem irresistible to others. You have a passionate heart and aren't afraid to share it with those you care about.

Exercise to Try: Breath of Fire Meditation

Wake up with a breath of fire meditation, giving you the boost you need without resorting to filling your body with toxins like caffeine. Yogis have taught this method of meditation for thousands of years, and the results speak for themselves. Your energy levels and productivity will increase, allowing you to tackle your challenges. Having a means of natural stimulation is a healthier alternative to artificial stimulants, and you'll feel stronger, clearer, and more powerful than those who have to depend on other means of getting their energy for the day.

How to Do It:

1. Begin by sitting in a cross-legged position. Make sure to sit up tall.

2. Place your hands on your knees with your palms facing upward. You can also place a hand on your belly, feeling it rise and fall as you breathe.

3. Inhale through your nose, allowing your belly to expand as you breathe in.

4. Without pausing, exhale forcefully through your nose, contracting your abdominal muscles as you do. Make sure the length of time you breathe in is the same as when you breathe out. Repeat this pattern until you become comfortable with it.

5. Maintain this rhythm, inhaling slowly and exhaling forcefully. Continue to repeat these actions multiple times for practice.

6. Next, speed up your breathing, inhaling and exhaling faster. Remember, your exhales should still be forceful and loud.

7. Repeat the faster breathing for 30 seconds.

Over time, as you become more accustomed to using the Breath of Fire breathing technique, you can try to do it for longer periods.

Willow

Willow Tree.

Title: The Observer

Birthdates: April 15 to May 12

Traits: Intuitive, Sympathetic, Calm

Compatibility: Ivy and Birch

You are someone who values honesty and integrity. Your sympathetic and generous nature is often on display since you are the type of person who prefers peace and love to drama and chaos. Not only are you intellectual, but you also have a great amount of emotional intelligence, capable of understanding how those around you are feeling, even if they don't tell you. You have a grounded perspective on life, seeing the reality of a situation but never resorting to cynicism. When dealing with others, you are extremely polite and kind. However, you also enjoy joking around with your friends and have a great sense of humor. When people are around you, they can't help but be cheered up and see the brighter side of things.

Exercise to Try: State of Stillness Meditation

Using the state of stillness meditation is a great remedy for anyone with difficulty sleeping. Spend the night tossing and turning, unable to calm your mind and relax your body. You can use this technique to grant you the peace necessary for a proper period of rest. This form of guided meditation will induce a state of stillness and relaxation that will ease your mind and release the tension from your body. Once you are able to drift off, you'll find yourself in a deep, unburdened sleep, enjoying the restoration granted by having a night of uninterrupted slumber. This will allow your mind and body to recover, ready to face the morning when you finally awaken.

How to Do It:

1. Lie down on your bed and find a comfortable position. Extend your legs out and allow your arms to rest alongside your body, turning your palms to face up.

2. Begin by scrunching and tightening your feet and toes, then relax them. Your muscles should contract and release. Do this multiple times, working any tension out of your feet.

3. Again, tighten your feet and toes as you inhale deeply, and then relax as you fully exhale.

4. Moving up your body, repeat the technique of contracting and releasing your muscles. Do it with your ankles, your legs, your hips and rear, your belly, your chest, your hands, your arms, your shoulders, your neck, and your face. Remember to continue with your breathing as you do this.

5. Complete three repetitions of tightening and relaxing your whole body.

6. After the final repetition, close your eyes, contracting every muscle in your body as you inhale. Upon exhaling, release your muscles, pushing out all the tension. Return your breathing to normal, and you should be able to fall asleep peacefully.

Hawthorn

Hawthorn Tree.
https://pixabay.com/es/photos/espino-floraci%c3%b3n-%c3%a1rbol-wet-4196348/

Title: The Illusionist

Birthdates: May 13 to June 9

Traits: Passionate, Fun, Secretive, Wily

Compatibility: Rowan and Ash

You are a person who has a lot more going on inside than you allow people to see. There is a great amount of passion and creativity within you; you are just searching for a constructive outlet. You tend to see the big picture, which grants you the ability to adapt to nearly any situation. It also lets you display a sense of maturity that shows you are intelligent and even-tempered. You're a naturally curious person, always seeking to learn new things. This makes you a great listener, and people feel comfortable divulging their deepest secrets. You have an ironic sense of humor, often picking up on subtleties and making insightful observations. However, this may be veiled in the form of jokes.

Exercise to Try: Fast Asleep Meditation Technique

The fast-asleep meditation technique helps to slow down a busy mind and helps you get to sleep quickly. You have plenty of responsibilities to take care of every single day, and you can't afford to waste a single moment of the night lying awake in bed, unable to push out the mental to-do lists or instinctive planning for the following morning. This meditation technique can help slow the chaos running through your head, allowing you to fall asleep fast. Maximizing the limited time you have to rest makes you more likely to wake up feeling refreshed.

How to Do It:

Start by scanning your body. This means taking notice of your breathing and the spots where your body is in contact with your bed. Beginning with your toes, mentally "turn off" any tension or movement in that part of your body. Let them go limp and keep them relaxed. Repeat this process for each part of your body, from the tips of your toes to the top of your head.

Begin counting your breaths as they alternate between inhales and exhales. Start by counting the first breath in as 1, then the following breath out as 2. When you inhale again, count 3; when you exhale, count 4. Continue doing this until you get to 10. This is to keep your focus on your breathing, allowing all other thoughts to melt away. If your mind wanders to other things, restart your counting at 1.

Oak

Oak Tree.

https://pixabay.com/es/photos/roble-%c3%a1rbol-bosque-prado-oto%c3%b1o-7468708/

Title: The Stabilizer

Birthdates: June 10 to July 7

Traits: Loyal, Peaceful, Courageous, Fair-Minded

Compatibility: Reed and Ash

You are someone who feels strongly about defending those who cannot speak up for themselves, acting as a champion of righteousness. Your sympathies will almost always lie with the underdog, as you believe they should be given a fair shot in life. Due to this, many people want to be your friend, and you have a large social network. There is a calming effect about your presence, as people feel safe and comfortable around you. You have great respect for history, using your knowledge of the past to gain insight into the future. Whenever you get a chance to spend time with your friends and family, you have a great time reminiscing with everyone.

Exercise to Try: Healing Waters Meditation

You can use the power of healing waters meditation to visualize and release any mental, emotional, or physical pain you are carrying. Anxiety, sadness, anger, and tension build up throughout the day, causing you to bear that weight as you attempt to go about your routine. Fortunately, the purifying relief of the healing waters technique will wash over you and flush that weight from your mind, body, and spirit.

How to Do It:

Find a comfortable place to sit down. You can then use an audio track or video guiding you through healing waters meditation, repeating the mantra when prompted and following the instructions, or you can read them to yourself. For the latter option, the following will serve as your guide:

(Speak out loud)

"I shall let the water soothe me and heal my pain in my mind, my body, and my soul. I have brought it all here right now so the healing waters can wash it away."

1. Settle your body and find your breath. Wiggle around a bit to release any tension and make yourself comfortable.

2. The next time you exhale, allow your shoulders to drop and relax your body.

3. Breathe in and out. Each time you do this, extend your breaths a little longer and breathe in a bit deeper.

4. Draw out the breaths and slow them down. Try to slow down your mind and your body as well.

5. Take a pause.

6. If you can feel any physical pain, try to pinpoint its origin. Visualize a warm hum being emitted from that spot.

7. Say out loud, *"This is my pain, and I reject it. Where there was pain, I feel only the healing energy of the sea."*

8. If you feel pain in your heart or mind, allow yourself to experience it at the moment. Do not cling to it; release it from you.

9. • (Say out loud, *"This is my pain, and I have set it free. Where there was pain, I feel only the rejuvenating power of the ocean."*

10. Take a pause.

11. Listen carefully for the sound of the water all around you. Picture the waves of the ocean racing across the sand, and then see them retreat back to the sea.

12. As you breathe in, imagine the waves washing through you. As you breathe out, imagine them ebbing and taking your pain with them back to the sea.

Holly

Holly Tree.
https://pixabay.com/es/photos/holly-tree-houx-stechpalme-acebo-1030595/

Title: The Ruler

Birthdates: July 8 to August 4

Traits: Leader, Confident, Noble

Compatibility: Elder and Ash

You have an air of nobility about you, and others view you as a respectable person. You are often looked to by others to provide leadership, and your natural confidence allows you to take on the mantle of leadership without hesitation. Failure is not an option for you, and you press forth when faced with obstacles, finding new and inventive ways to overcome them. In the rare instance that you experience a setback, it only spurs you on to work harder and refocus your efforts on reaching your objective. You are organized and goal-oriented even when spending your time on leisurely activities. This can be intimidating to outsiders, but those within your inner circle know that you are also a warm and generous person.

Exercise to Try: Mindfulness Meditation

Mindfulness meditation can help you be fully present in the moment. You should always take some time to focus on where you are and what you're doing in the here and now rather than thinking about the past or the future. This prevents you from becoming overwhelmed by your responsibilities or the drama in your life. The more you worry about other things while going about your normal routine, the greater the chance that something slips your mind or you make a mistake that could've been avoided if you'd been paying closer attention. Take notice of your thoughts, emotions, and senses as you are currently experiencing them.

How to Do It:

1. Take a seat. Find a place that offers a stable, solid surface. This can be a chair, a bench, a cushion, or anything else, as long as you're not perching or hanging back.

2. Observe what your legs are doing. If you're on a cushion or sitting on the floor, comfortably cross your legs in front of you. If you are experienced with any seated yoga postures, use those instead. If you're sitting on a chair, bench, or other raised surface, make sure the soles of your feet are touching the floor.

3. Straighten your upper body. Don't stiffen up, though. The spine has natural curvature to it, so allow it to be there. Let your head and shoulders rest on top of your vertebrae comfortably.

4. Position your upper arms parallel to your upper body. Then allow your hands to drop onto the tops of your legs. Don't try to force them into the right spot; as long as your upper arms are at your sides, your hands should naturally land correctly in your lap. If you rest them too far forward, it will cause you to hunch. If you rest them too far back, it will make you stiff. Imagine you're tuning the strings of an instrument; they shouldn't be too tight or too loose.

5. Drop your chin a bit and gently allow your gaze to fall downward. You can lower your eyelids. Should you feel the need, you can

close them completely, but it's not necessary to do this while meditating. You can just let whatever your eyes are looking at remain there, focusing on it.

6. Remain in this position for a few moments. Relax and pay attention to your breathing or the sensations you feel within your body.

7. Follow your breath and feel it as it moves in and out. If you want, you can emphasize exhaling more and leave a brief pause after inhaling. Draw your attention to the actual physical sensation of breathing. Feel the air passing through your nose or mouth and the rise and fall of your belly or chest. Pick a focal point, and as you take each breath, make a mental note when you breathe in and breathe out.

8. Your mind may wander from your breathing and go to other places. That's okay. It's not necessary to block out your thoughts or eliminate them from your head. Whenever you catch your mind wandering, be it for a few seconds or a few minutes, simply return your attention to your breathing.

9. Practice taking a pause before making any physical adjustments, like if you need to move to avoid a cramp or scratch an irritating itch. You can then shift at whatever moment you choose, allowing for some space between what you are experiencing and when you take deliberate action.

10. If you find your mind is constantly wandering, that's okay, too. Rather than grappling with or engaging those thoughts, practice observing them without the need to react. Just sit there and pay attention to your breathing. It might be difficult to keep returning your attention to only your breathing, but that's all there is to do. Come back to it as often as necessary without judgments or expectations.

11. Whenever you're ready, lift your gaze back up, and open your eyes if they are closed. Take a second to listen for any sounds in the environment around you. Pay attention to how your body feels at this very moment. Pay attention to your thoughts and emotions. Before standing up, allow yourself a minute to decide how you'd like to approach the rest of your day.

Hazel

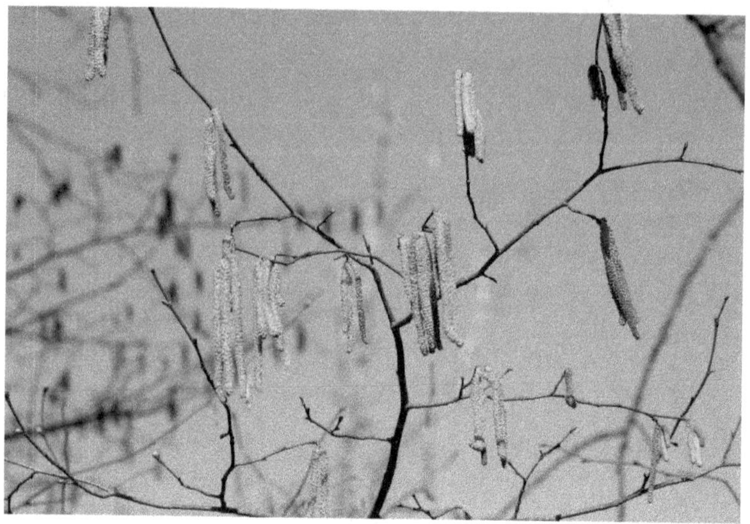

Hazel Tree.
https://pixabay.com/es/photos/color-avellana-%c3%a1rbol-rama-figura-4837464/

Title: The Knower

Birthdates: August 5 to September 1

Traits: Intelligent, Loyal, Confident

Compatibility: Rowan and Hawthorn

You tend to be introverted, preferring quiet solitude to loud social settings. However, you also have a great personality, which people find very attractive once they get to know you. You are a voracious reader, and you keep up with current events, making you a reliable information source. Since you are very intelligent, you can often figure out the best course of action to take in any given situation, but you are never conceited about your capabilities. You are fiercely loyal to your loved ones and will go to the ends of the Earth to protect them. Despite your success, you are always willing to improve yourself, acknowledging your faults and working to be a better person.

Exercise to Try: De-stressing Meditation

De-stressing meditation is a short yet efficient method for centering yourself. Try using it before going to an event you've been dreading or after a long, stressful day. No matter how minor things that irritate or upset you might seem, they can accumulate over time, snowballing into a massive weight that crashes into you and knocks you off your feet. Fortunately, de-stressing meditation can help you get through whatever challenges stand in your way. You can overcome any obstacles by keeping a clear head and a light heart.

How to Do It:

1. Get into a position that's comfortable for you. Decide where and how you will sit. Some people prefer sitting in a chair, and others like to sit cross-legged on the floor or another large, flat surface. Wherever you choose, you should be somewhere where you can fully relax while remaining alert and aware.

2. Make sure you are using the correct posture. Sitting up straight is easier to stay awake during extended meditation sessions. Suppose you remember to start each session by first adopting the correct posture. In that case, your body will become accustomed to naturally sitting in this position as you advance to spending long periods meditating.

3. During a meditation session, try to remain mindful that you maintain the correct posture. If you notice that you're slumping your shoulders, take the opportunity to make corrections and sit back up straight. Keeping your body from using incorrect posture helps to prevent unnecessary soreness after extended meditation.

4. If you decide to sit in a chair, position yourself toward the front of the seat, and plant both feet firmly on the floor. This helps with improving your posture and allows you to concentrate on your meditation practice.

5. Once in a comfortable position, cast your gaze into the distance and lower your eyelids, but don't close your eyes yet. Your jaw should remain slack as you do this. Relax the muscles in your face while your eyes remain slightly open. After relaxing your facial muscles, you can close your eyes to begin meditating. Don't squeeze them shut tight, though. If you feel the muscles in your face tense up, slowly reopen your eyes and repeat the relaxation of your face before closing them again.

6. At this point in your meditation session, the goal is to relax every part of your body. You may feel tension in areas that tend to get tight, so take a deep breath in, hold it for a count of five seconds, and then breathe out slowly, allowing your body to relax completely.

7. Try to set your thoughts aside. Don't try to control the thoughts themselves; instead, control how much power you give them. There's no need to ignore or suppress your thoughts, but try to remain calm, take note of them, and then focus on your breathing to help you return to the moment. This practice isn't merely useful for meditation; it can aid you throughout the day, teaching you how to let things go and remain focused on the task at hand.

8. Don't become too flustered if you find your thoughts running out of control. There is no judgment here. Simply take the time to observe that you let your thoughts carry you away, and then refocus and return to your breathing. Continue to put aside any thoughts that may pop into your head. The longer you practice, the more time will pass when your mind remains quiet before your thoughts return.

9. Remember to give yourself time to adjust to your meditation practice. Don't put too much pressure on yourself to get everything right, as this can end up causing you more stress than it relieves. It's unreasonable to expect that your meditation sessions will all be perfect. Putting yourself under that kind of pressure can make meditation feel like a chore, and it'll be less likely that you'll want to continue with it in the future.

10. Try starting with shorter 5-minute meditation sessions and slowly work your way up to longer ones. When you feel like you've gotten the hang of the 5-minute sessions, you can try doing a 10-minute session. Then move on to a 15-minute session. Keep adding another 5 minutes until you can meditate regularly for 30-minute sessions.

11. The more you practice your meditation, the easier it becomes, and it can be an effective stress relief tool. You should emerge from a 30-minute meditation session feeling refreshed, relaxed, and rejuvenated. If you meditate in the morning, you'll be ready to start your day with plenty of energy, and if you meditate at night, it will allow you to let go of the tension so you can fall asleep without a struggle.

12. It can be a good idea to set goals for yourself while meditating and keeping track of your time. If you're not used to emptying your mind and relaxing, every minute that passes might feel like an eternity, even when you've barely started the session. Constantly

thinking about how much time has passed can become distracting, and if you're worrying about meditating for too long, it'll defeat the purpose of trying to de-stress.

13. The best way to handle this is to set a timer so you can be confident that you won't throw off your entire schedule. You can also play some soothing sounds or gentle music to help get you into the right headspace for meditating. This can also aid you in avoiding too many intrusive thoughts, as you can focus on the music if tracking your breathing isn't helping. Eventually, you'll get to the point where you won't need the timer, as your body will naturally become accustomed to relaxing for a set amount of time.

Vine

Vine Tree.

https://pixabay.com/es/photos/uvas-fruta-vino-planta-vid-1696921/

Title: The Equalizer

Birthdates: September 2 to September 29

Traits: Charming, Elegant, Loving

Compatibility: Willow and Hazel

You are someone who enjoys the finer things in life, never hesitant to indulge in luxuries. At the same time, you are also very generous, spreading your good fortune so others can enjoy life with you. You never expect to have things handed to you, and you are always willing to work hard to pay for your expensive tastes. Your compassionate nature means you can often see things from other people's perspectives, but this can also make you a bit unpredictable and indecisive since you will believe that both sides have a point. You also don't like conflict or confrontation, preferring to remain neutral in such situations. Although you can become withdrawn if someone breaks your heart, you always conduct yourself with poise and charm.

Exercise to Try: Beauty Sleep Meditation

The beauty sleep meditation is meant to help you enter a state of deep relaxation. It will bring your inner radiance to the forefront and allow you to get your beauty sleep. Using this meditation technique can rejuvenate your soul, reinvigorate your mind, and restore your body to a place where you can connect with your inner bliss. There is no better time to practice this form of meditation than while lying in bed; you will have an easier time entering a peaceful slumber if you follow this guide.

How to Do It:

1. Lay down in bed and get comfortable. Once you're set, enter a place in your mind where you can disconnect from the outside world.

2. Let go of the stresses and turmoil that have accumulated throughout the day. Even if you had a good day, let go of it. The day is over, and it's time to focus on the peace ahead as you drift off to sleep.

3. Take a deep breath in and slowly breathe out. Pay attention to the way you feel at this moment. Breathe in and out, releasing the tension in your body until you feel the weight of the day has been lifted.

4. Close your eyes and surrender to the calm, loving energy within you. There is a radiance to your soul, so allow it to shine.

5. Remind yourself that you are strong. That you are powerful. That you are beautiful.

6. Accept the peace and renewal that comes with a good night's sleep. Focus on your breathing and let everything else just melt away.

7. Surrender your consciousness to the somnolent reveries of your dreams. You are relaxed and serene, allowing yourself a beautiful night of re-energizing sleep.

Ivy

Ivy Plant.
https://pixabay.com/es/photos/bosque-hiedra-tronco-de-arbol-5159093/

Title: The Survivor

Birthdates: September 30 to October 27

Traits: Determined, Brave, Kind

Compatibility: Ash and Oak

You have a unique personality that can give people pause, but your sharp wit and brilliance usually win them over. Once you become friends with someone, you will cherish them for life. As a dreamer, it can be difficult for you to face reality, but you possess the determination to actually follow through on your more far-fetched goals. During times of struggle, you refuse to complain and press onward with quiet grace. You often turn to spirituality and faith to see you through any difficulties. You are quick to lend your aid to others, sympathizing with their problems due to your own experiences. While you aren't an obvious extrovert, you can be very charismatic when you choose to be, dazzling people with your cleverness and charm.

Exercise to Try: Complete Release Body Scan Meditation

A complete release body scan meditation helps to prepare your mind, body, and spirit to get a healthy amount of sleep. You will make a connection with each part of your body and leave the problems of your waking life behind. This technique can help you evolve your daily meditations to a more effective approach, gaining benefits to a greater extent. Fully scanning your body to ensure a proper release of tension is essential to feeling renewed and at ease when you have finished meditating.

How to Do It:

1. Sit in a chair or lay down in a comfortable position.

2. Take a deep breath in and hold it, then let the breath out. Keep your shoulders steady as you breathe; they shouldn't be going up and down. Slow down your breathing and feel it in your belly. Allow it to expand and contract. Picture a balloon being inflated and deflated each time you inhale and exhale.

3. Be aware of your body, drawing your attention to the sensations within it. Begin at your feet and move upward until you reach your head. As your focus passes across each body part, take note of what you can feel in them. If you feel any soreness or pain, allow yourself to accept it and how you feel about it. Try to breathe through these issues. When you're ready, move along to the next part of your body.

4. Keep scanning until you've scanned your whole body. Be mindful of any tension you're holding. Often, your neck or back will be some of the primary areas retaining tension. Make a mental note of anywhere with tightness, pressure, or pain. After noticing any discomfort, visualize yourself sending healing energy to those parts of your body. It can be a great method of relieving tension at the moment.

5. Try to recognize the areas where you tend to hold stress. This can be useful even when you're not meditating. Anytime you notice yourself feeling that tension, let your body relax and send a wave of positive energy to release it while controlling your breathing. Always practice mindfulness to make sure you are treating your body with the care it deserves.

Reed

Reed Plant.

https://pixabay.com/es/photos/carrizo-semillas-silvergrass-5110318/

Title: The Inquisitor

Birthdates: October 28 to November 24

Traits: Compassionate, Honest, Curious

Compatibility: Ash and Oak

You are an honorable person with a strong sense of integrity, loathing dishonesty, and disloyalty. Others see you as someone they can confide in since you are easy to talk to about important matters, and they know you can keep a secret. You like to explore deeper into subjects that catch your interest, and your ability to sniff out the truth makes you a natural investigator or journalist. Your curiosity also means you enjoy learning about gossip, scandals, and other hidden stories. Once you reach the truth, you are able to quickly understand the motivation behind it. You also desire to set the record straight since you hate when people are blamed for things they didn't do or weren't involved in.

Exercise to Try: Rainbow Hypnosis Meditation

Rainbow hypnosis meditation is a useful method to help you ease your way into sleep by going through each color of the rainbow. It lets you utilize the power of hypnosis to send your mind into a deep, peaceful state of restfulness. As you take the voyage through the vast ocean of colors, it can enhance the way you dream, ensuring that you will wake up feeling restored and energized.

How to Do It:

1. Lie down flat on your back.

2. Take a deep breath in through your nose, and then let it out through your mouth. Do this three times.

3. Shut your eyes or let your eyelids fall about halfway closed, and choose a focal point for your gaze.

4. Visualize yourself floating on a lake. Imagine the warm, still water surrounding your body and gently carrying you across its surface.

5. Picture yourself looking up at the sky as you float across the water. You feel warm and safe, immersed in the calming waters of the lake. It gently moves you along until you see a rainbow above you.

6. Imagine the rainbow reaching across the sky. It stretches down to the lake, allowing you to float into it. As you move across the rainbow, you can feel the colors wash across your body, relaxing your muscles and infusing you with positive energy.

7. The color red brings you radiant warmth. It feels like standing on a fire that doesn't burn but sends restorative energy from your head to toe. Breathe in and out, allowing yourself to be engulfed by the red energy of the rainbow.

8. The color orange ignites your passion. Allow yourself to think about a subject or activity that brings you joy. Take notice of that feeling and sustain it, letting you feel that joy deep in your heart. Breathe in and out, infusing your body with the orange energy of the rainbow.

9. The color yellow encourages positivity. Let it expel any negativity from your mind, focusing on the things in your life for which you are thankful. Look for the bright side when thinking about your troubles. Breathe in and out, shining with the light of the yellow energy of the rainbow.

10. The color green bathes you in rejuvenating power. Imagine yourself as a tree, your branches bare as the day's stress has sapped your energy. This restorative power nourishes your roots, and fresh leaves begin to grow until you have been renewed. Breathe in and out, feeding on the green energy of the rainbow.

11. The color blue sparks your creativity. It inspires you to conceive new and exciting ideas, painting a magnificent picture with the palette of your mind. Give yourself permission to dream. Breathe

in and out, indulging in your imagination of the blue energy of the rainbow.

12. The color indigo embodies your wisdom. Allow it to give your mind clarity so you can look at any obstacles in your life and make sound decisions about how to deal with them. Use it to remind yourself to consider your experiences and draw forth the lessons they taught you. Breathe in and out, enlightening yourself with the indigo energy of the rainbow.

13. The color purple offers you strength. As it fills your body, it fortifies your muscles, invigorates your spirit, and reinforces your mind. There is no challenge you cannot overcome and no problem that is too difficult for you to solve. Breathe in and out, bolstering your being with the purple energy of the rainbow.

14. As the final color finishes moving through your body, envision the rainbow gently setting you back down into the water. You float all the way back to your bed, coming to rest and feeling the tranquility as a result of your meditation.

Elder

Elder Tree.

https://pixabay.com/es/photos/mayor-planta-%c3%a1rbol-fruta-rama-398009/

Title: The Seeker

Birthdates: November 25 to December 23

Traits: Ambitious, Thoughtful, Loyal

Compatibility: Holly and Alder

You regard your freedom very highly and enjoy being spontaneous. You're a bit of a thrill-seeker, always ready for a good adventure. This zest for life often spreads to others, and they love being around you because of it. There is a big world out there, and you have the ambition to see as much of it as you can. You are also kind and thoughtful, being considerate of other people's feelings and lending assistance when needed. Some people might think that you're shallow or ditzy, but you are actually quite intelligent and philosophical, as your wide range of life experiences has exposed you to many unique perspectives about life.

Exercise to Try: Yoga Nidra Meditation

Yoga Nidra does not focus on relaxation but will still result in you feeling relaxed as a natural side-effect of this meditation technique. It takes you on a journey through every layer of your consciousness until you reach the inner sanctum of your soul. Opening your mind and sweeping away your negative preconceptions and emotions helps you find a more balanced perspective in your life. Self-awareness and self-inquiry allow you to open your heart and find a place for personal acceptance.

How to Do It:

1. Find somewhere with no distractions. This means no noise or visual stimulation. A darkened room or sleep mask will be the best way to block out any light, and if you can't find a quiet place, try earplugs or noise-canceling headphones.

2. Start by lying down on a bed, blanket, or yoga mat, placing a pillow beneath you to support your head, neck, spine, and lower back. Make sure that you're comfortable before you begin meditating.

3. Make sure that your arms are resting on the ground, away from your sides. Your hands should be roughly even with your waist, with your palms facing up. Your legs should also be resting flat on the ground but spread just enough so that your feet line up with your shoulders.

4. Stay completely still and silent. This will aid you in relaxing your mind and body. Slow down your breathing until you are taking gentle breaths without any effort. Close your eyes, allowing your eyelids to rest atop your eyeballs, don't squeeze them shut.

5. Visualize a specific part of your body. It doesn't matter which one; just make sure to focus solely on this body part, avoiding any other distractions. Use your senses to observe what you're feeling in that

part of your body. Acknowledge these sensations before moving on to another area.

6. Repeat the previous step until you've gone through every part of your body. Then do the same process for your body as a whole. Envision yourself surrounded by a warm, calming aura. At this point, you should be fully relaxed and relieved of all your tension.

7. Begin to return to an active state. Start by moving your fingers and wiggling them around for a few seconds. Take a deep breath in, hold it for 5 seconds, and then let it out again. Open your eyes and move into a sitting position.

8. Stretch your arms and drop your chin, letting your head hang forward. Roll it from side to side a couple of times. Once you are ready, get to your feet and return to your daily routine.

Chapter 7: Celtic Animal Magic

Celtic Druids and shamans have a strong connection to many types of animals. Their affinity for nature means they view wild creatures and noble beasts as powerful symbolic figures. They often look to the earth, water, and sky for animals to teach them lessons about living in harmony with the environment. In some cases, this reverence for animals evolves into religious worship of them. Some hold a higher position in Celtic society, and certain powers and traits are associated with the most important animals.

Some animals have special significance in Celtic culture.
https://pixabay.com/es/vectors/c%c3%a9ltico-simbolos-animales-gato-40393/

Animals in Celtic Culture

There are many instances of animal symbolism in Celtic art. The illuminated manuscripts created during the medieval era contain beautifully crafted illustrations of creatures representing major religious figures. In the Book of Kells, three of the four authors of the New Testament Gospels are shown as animals significant to Celtic culture - Matthew is depicted as a man, while a lion stands in for Mark, a calf for Luke, and an eagle for John.

The British, Scottish, and Irish aristocracy members include animal symbolism as part of their coat of arms. Many inns and pubs adopt names that include animals, such as the Old Ram in Tivetshall St Mary, the Packhorse and Pig in London, and the Stag's Head in Dublin. Coins minted in Ireland during the 20th century had bulls, wolfhounds, salmon, horses, and Irish hares on their backs. Celtic mythology is rife with instances where people are transformed into wild creatures or animals possessing unique powers that aid their masters in overcoming obstacles.

Animal Symbolism

The animals that have special significance in Celtic culture include the following:

Horses

Horses are considered noble and intelligent creatures, renowned for their speed, endurance, vitality, and beauty. In addition to their revered position in Celtic society, they also had an air of mystery about them. They have a strong connection to the night, particularly in that the term "nightmare" includes "mare," the word for a female horse. This was associated with the goddess Epona, a major figure in Celtic mythology worshiped as the protector of horses and other related creatures.

Besides being one of the most common transportation methods throughout pre-industrialized history, horses were also a regular sight on battlefields. They would carry commanders, archers, and cavalry soldiers, as well as pulling chariots that often gave their riders an advantage in combat. Horse racing was a popular form of entertainment, and many leisure activities included them as a primary component, such as jousting, polo, and fox hunting.

Snakes and Serpents

Despite the well-known myth about St. Patrick driving all the snakes out of Ireland, both snakes and serpents have a long and complicated history with Celtic society. They are said to represent rebirth, creation, and healing. The many winding rivers, streams, and tributaries are described as being serpentine, and snakes are often depicted as a conduit between the spiritual realm and the physical world. Many Celtic symbols, like the triskelion, resemble three coiling serpents.

In Celtic mythology, there is a being known as the Ram-Horned Serpent or Ram-Headed Snake, who often accompanied other gods, particularly in artwork dating from the early Iron Age. The Ram-Horned Serpent was most frequently a companion for Toutatis or Lugh, both chief gods of the religion. There is an association between snakes and the solar wheel, which is evocative of Jörmungandr, the World Serpent from Norse mythology whose entire body encircles the Earth, or Ouroboros from Greek mythology, who is shown eating its own tail and represents the cycle of life, death, and rebirth.

Deer

Deer, especially stags, are connected to Cernunnos, the antlered god of hunting and nature. Does are usually seen as emblematic of birth, renewal, and innocence, while their adult counterparts are associated with virility, abundance, and strength. Antlers are often viewed as a trophy for hunters, and some people can make decent money finding antlers shed by deer in the wild. They are an animal that symbolizes growth in the spring and harvest in the autumn.

White stags appear in Celtic artwork, literature, and mythology. They are said to have come from the Otherworld, and their appearance heralds a period of great transformation that will soon occur. This change can be good or bad, but it is usually an overall positive experience, even if it doesn't seem so at first. Some folklore depicts a person spotting a white stag as presaging a major shift in their fortunes, suddenly gaining a major influx of money and resources.

Dogs and Hounds

As with many cultures, dogs and hounds are considered beloved pets and companions in Celtic society. They remain ever faithful to their masters and never waver in their devotion, loyalty, and love. Dogs are very protective and possess a strong intuition about danger, so keeping them by one's side is always safer than journeying alone. Most dogs will guard their master with their life, and many owners are equally willing to risk their lives for their pets.

Salmon

The ancient Celtic people used salmon as a symbol of knowledge. They represent the accumulation of that knowledge, a vast network of people and experiences that builds over time, all flowing toward the next generation. This is illustrated by the way the rivers, streams, and tributaries where salmon swim all flow to the ocean. Their importance to Celtic culture was so great that the Irish even began minting coins bearing the image of a salmon on its reverse side.

Birds

There is a wide variety of birds that hold significance in Celtic culture. Each type has been assigned its own characteristics, and it would be useful to list them for you now:

- **Ravens:** They are associated with death. Druids often used them in augury, and when flying over a battlefield, they were believed to be a god incarnate.

- **Crows:** They are associated with death, just like ravens. However, crows are generally seen as a negative omen.

- **Cranes:** these represent a false transformation, i.e., claiming you will change when you only superficially alter your actions or behaviors.

- **Peacocks:** They are a symbol of purity.

- **Herons:** are considered ideal for representing loyalty, fidelity, and marriage since they mate for life.

- **Eagles:** skilled hunters with keen eyes, making them an obvious symbol for those who embody similar qualities. They are also considered a noble animal, but one that remains very dangerous.

Finding Your Spirit Animal

Suppose you want to find a spirit animal that can symbolize your personality and character traits. In that case, you can do this in several ways. The most common way involves some soul-searching and careful attention to the details in your life. This process involves the following steps:

- Look to nature and observe the world around you. Watch how different animals behave, how they move, and what they do. The longer you study them, the more familiar you will become with their personalities and the characteristics they embody.

- Learn about your lineage. Depending on who your ancestors were, you might already have a connection to a particular animal without realizing it. Certain animals are very closely linked to a specific culture or group of people.

- Be mindful of your dreams. Your unconscious mind is always making connections that your waking mind doesn't. It can be easy to forget your dreams, so keep a dream journal beside your bed and quickly jot down an entry whenever an animal appears in one of your dreams.

- Keep an eye out for repeat encounters with the same animal. This can be either a real, living animal or just a symbol of it that you find popping up time and time again. There is a good chance that if you notice one type of animal constantly appearing as you go about your day, the universe is trying to tell you something.

- Meditate on the subject. During a meditation session, clear your mind of all thoughts and let your intentions about finding your spirit animal be known. You may discover your thoughts suddenly turn toward a specific animal. This could be your spirit animal guiding you to it.

- Go on a vision quest. Find a shaman willing to lead you through a vision quest to find your spirit animal. This could involve entering a trance-like state, but more often than not, you will only need to follow the shaman's advice on how to find what you seek.

Chapter 8: Earth Magic Rituals

Earth magic is the foundation of all shamanistic wisdom. The power within the earth runs deep, and knowing how to tap into it is a skill most shamans possess. However, you can harness some of the magic contained within the earth for yourself. If you're serious about learning to use earth magic, you must dedicate yourself to practice. It takes a great amount of strength and willpower to wield it properly. If you haven't trained yourself to handle this potent energy, it can end up costing you dearly.

Earth magic is the foundation of all shamanistic wisdom.

Earth Magic and Ley Lines

Ley lines are avenues of energy created by the alignment of magically-significant landmarks. These landmarks are set around a location that is infused with energy, and that energy can be directed toward another landmark some distance away. The path linking these connected sites serves as a conduit through which the energy is sent, strengthening the connection between them. Training individuals such as shamans and Druids can tap into the ley lines to help increase the effectiveness of their spells, charms, and rituals.

Celtic Prayers

Here are some prayers that you can recite to help you reinforce your mind, body, and spirit for the purpose of using earth magic:

Prayers to the Earth Mother, Part 1

"Earth Mother

receive in your great bounty

all the blood that has poured over me,

the sorrow that has mired me down.

Let me be free,

so flowers and trees may sprout from me to the heavens,

so birds may come and perch on my wings

and sing their eternal song of gratitude.

Dear Earth Mother,

may your bounty feed the downtrodden,

may you comfort each knee and forehead pressed into your layers,

may la Virgen de Guadalupe's roses flourish

and the trees that become crosses be strong,

may your robes encompass stars, moon, and ocean, day and night,

and hold me in its folds, Earth Mother. O our Mother the Earth, blessed is your name.

Prayer to the Earth Mother, Part 2

"Blessed are your fields and forests, your rocks and mountains, your grasses and trees and flowers, and every green and growing thing.

Blessed are your streams and lakes and rivers, the oceans where our life began, and all your waters that sustain our bodies and refresh our souls.

Blessed is the air we breathe, your atmosphere that surrounds us and binds us to every living thing.

Blessed are all creatures who walk along your surface or swim in your waters or fly through your air, for they are all our relatives.

Blessed are all people who share this planet, for we are all one family, and the same spirit moves through us all.

Blessed is the sun, our day star, bringer of the morning and the heat of summer, giver of light and life.

Blessed is the moon, our night lamp, ruler of the tides, protector of all women, and guardian of our dreams.

Blessed are the stars and planets, the time-keepers, who fill our nights with beauty and our hearts with awe.

O Great Spirit, whose voice we hear in the wind and whose face we see in the morning sun, blessed is your name.

Help us to remember that you are everywhere, and teach us the way of peace."

Prayer to Lugh

"Great, Lugh!

Master of artisans,

leader of craftsmen,

patron of smiths,

I call upon you and honor you this day.

You the many skills and talents,

I ask you to shine upon me and

bless me with your gifts.

Give me strength in skill,

make my hands and mind deft,

and shine light upon my talents.

O mighty Lugh,

I thank you for your blessings."

Prayer to Epona

"Hail Epona Rigantona! Rigantona Epona Hail!

Epona of Horses, I praise you!

Rigantona of the Land, I praise you!

Epona of Sovereignty, I praise you!

Rigantona of Journeys, I praise you!

Epona of Stables, I praise you!

Rigantona of the Otherworld, I praise you!

Epona, Great Mother, I praise you!

Rigantona of the Singing Birds, I praise you!

Epona Rigantona, guide, guardian, and teacher, I praise you!

Epona of Horses, I honor you!

Rigantona of the Land, I honor you!

Epona of Sovereignty, I honor you!

Rigantona of Journeys, I honor you!

Epona of Stables, I honor you!

Rigantona of the Otherworld, I honor you!

Epona, Great Mother, I honor you!

Rigantona of the Singing Birds, I honor you!

Epona Rigantona, guide, guardian, and teacher, I honor you!

Epona of Horses, I thank you for your presence in my life.

Rigantona of the Land, I thank you for the stability in my life.

Epona of Sovereignty, I thank you for the choices you bring to my life.

Rigantona of Journeys, I thank you for your guidance through my life.

Epona of Stables, I thank you for the security in my life.

Rigantona of the Otherworld, I thank you for the mysteries in my life.

Epona, Great Mother, I thank you for your nurturing presence in my life.

Rigantona of the Singing Birds, I thank you for the beauty you bring to my life.

Epona Rigantona, guide, guardian, and teacher, I thank you for being with me through my life.

Hail Epona Rigantona! Rigantona Epona Hail!"

Creating a Celtic Altar

You can set up a Celtic altar to give yourself a permanent place to practice magic and commune with the gods. The first thing you need to do is decide if you want it to be indoors or outdoors. While having an altar outside will allow you to have a stronger connection to nature, it can be limiting if you live somewhere with frequent inclement weather, especially during the colder part of the year. An indoor altar has the benefit of being accessible at all times. Still, you will have to work harder to forge that connection to nature.

Choose which direction you want your altar to face. Most pagan altars face either north or northeast. Some practitioners of pagan religions that have a Christian influence will face their altars to the east because that's where the sun rises. It's also the traditional direction that many Christian churches are built to face.

Pick a surface or object on which you want to create your altar. This can be anything, from a table to a desk or a piece of furniture. Window sills can also work. If you want, you can even build something from scratch with a few pieces of wood. The important thing is that it has a flat surface and enough room to set up all the components of the altar.

Gather the items and objects you plan to place on your altar. Common options include candles, energy crystals, divination tools, statues or icons of a favored deity, totems of animals, or trinkets with personal significance. At this juncture, you should also decide which colors you want your altar to be. Blue, green, purple, silver, and gold are popular colors, as they often represent the deities and other powers involved in shamanism and Druidry.

When you're ready to set up your altar, get a cloth or cover in the color of your choice and place it over the surface you will use. Now it's time to actually add the items to the altar.

The right side of the altar will be the god's side, where you will place the objects associated with masculine traits. These can be statues or icons of a god, candles with warmer colors like red, orange, yellow, or gold, and totems of male animals, like stags, rams, or lions.

The left side is the goddess' side and will be reserved for objects with feminine traits. These can be statues or icons of a goddess, candles with cooler colors, like green, blue, purple, or silver, and totems of female animals, such as does, ewes, or lionesses.

The middle is where you will place the rest of the objects that are neutral and have no gendered traits. Common items placed in the middle are athames, wands, stones, or a Book of Shadows. After placing the last of the objects, you will be done setting up your altar.

Making a Sacred Space in the Forest

Making a sacred space in the forest is a fairly simple task. All you need is some salt, a small statue, a totem, icon, or picture, and a handful of herbs. Enter the forest and choose a spot with which you feel a connection. Make a rough outline using the salt of the space you want to sanctify. This doesn't need to be very big, just big enough to sit comfortably inside. Crush the herbs up in your hands and scatter them around the space. Finally, place your statue, totem, icon, or picture down within the sanctified area. You can recite prayers and blessings, perform rituals, or cast spells and charms from here. Being so close to nature means you will have an easier time drawing on the earth to aid your magic.

Cleansing and Consecration

If you need to cleanse a location or object, there are some good options to choose from:

- Bury the object in the earth, a bowl of salt, or a sack of cornmeal.

- Burn some incense while walking around the location being cleansed, dispersing its smoke throughout the area.

- Submerge the object in salt water, or fill a spray bottle with salt water and spritz it around the room.

- Purify an object over the flame of a candle, or place it within a fire.

- Fill a bowl or basin with blessed water and let it sit within a location needing cleansing, allowing the negative energy to be drawn into the water (make sure you dispose of the water outside and well away from any homes).

- Use a besom or a blessed broom to sweep away the negative energy.

- If you need to consecrate an item or the ground for performing rituals, you can try these options:

- Using cleansed oils, anoint the items by rubbing the oils across them.

- Consecrate the area using the elements. Perform a ritual involving earth, fire, water, and air. Try lighting a candle, sprinkling some salt, pouring out water, and burning some incense, so the smoke carries into the sky.

- Recite a prayer over the item or ground and make clear your intentions to dedicate the use of the item or space to your chosen deity.

Invoking Awen

Awen is the concept in Welsh mythology that serves as the spark of inspiration and creative energy for poets, bards, and other artists. You can invoke its personification to act as a muse for your artistic endeavors. To invoke Awen, recite the following prayer:

"Hear my words, hear my song

I will sing it to you all day long

Give me a melody, give me a verse

Guide my hand as I rehearse

My heart is heavy as I beg to thee

Draw forth the music, set it free

The wolf howls, the horse neighs

Light the spark that will grow into a blaze

There is power in every word

Don't let this song go unheard

In one voice, we call upon your grace

Take me into your warm embrace

Lose my song like an arrow from a bow

These words are meant for all to know."

Moon Water

You can use moon water in a variety of rituals, spells, and charms. It is a type of blessed water infused with the moon's healing and purification powers. Making it is a very simple process and doesn't take much effort.

All you need to do is follow these steps:

1. Choose the type of container you want to use. It should be made of glass so as not to interfere with the moon's energy while also preventing any of its power from escaping. Jars, jugs, or bottles generally work best. If you want to keep out anything from the environment that might fall into the water, use a container with a secure lid.

2. Fill the container with water. Fresh rainwater is preferable since it's natural and pure. Tap water is usually run through a treatment plant, so it can be contaminated with undesirable chemicals and pollutants. However, if you would like to drink your moon water, use bottled spring water.

3. Place your container of water in direct moonlight. This can be either inside or outside, as long as there aren't any obstructions between your water and the moon.

4. Recite a prayer over the water. It doesn't need to be anything too extensive. Something simple like, "Goddess of the moon, bless this water with your radiant light."

5. Place a crystal on top of the container to amplify the energy infusing the water. Amethyst, citrine, clear quartz, or moonstone are all great choices.

6. Leave the container sitting in the moonlight overnight. Let it soak under the moon for several nights for stronger moon water. Once you're satisfied that you've let it charge with enough energy, your moon water will be ready to use.

Sacred Trees and Plants

Here is a list of the sacred trees and plants important to Celtic earth magic:

Alder

Alder is a deciduous tree with serrated leaves and bearing catkins. It is believed to be able to hide and protect people from danger. The traits associated with it are protection, strength, confidence, and determination.

Apple

Apple trees are considered sacred in many cultures. It gets its name from the fruit it bears. The traits associated with it are good health and happiness.

Ash

Ash is noted for having hardwood with a straight grain. It is considered a symbol of power, sturdiness, and immortality. If you place leaves from an ash tree beneath your pillow, it is said to stimulate prophetic dreams.

Birch

Birch is a thin-leaved hardwood tree whose bark was used by heroic figures in Celtic mythology to write messages using Ogham. It symbolizes rebirth, growth, and new beginnings.

Blackthorn

Blackthorn is a winter tree. It has white flowers that grow before the leaves come in during the spring. Unfortunately, it has a poor reputation, as it represents black magic and the Crone facet of the Triple Goddess.

Broom

Broom is a shrub whose flowers can be used to make yellow dye. It represents healing and royalty, as it was the official emblem of Geoffrey of Anjou, father of the English king Henry II.

Cedar

Cedar trees have evergreen leaves and wood that carry a distinctive scent. It was popular with the Celtic people from Continental Europe, who used its oil as a preservative. It symbolizes nobility, strength, and greatness.

Elder

Elder plants, also known as elderberries, were used by the ancient Celtic people in cooking recipes, spells, rituals, and festival celebrations. It is believed that they would rub the juices from the elderberries on their cheeks to make them look redder, similar to how someone would use rouge today.

Elm

Elm is a tree with slightly fibrous, tan-colored wood that has a slight sheen. It is closely associated with the Otherworld, and many of the forests in the British Isles are made up mainly of elms. The wood from these trees has an interlocking grain that makes it highly resistant to splitting, causing it to be greatly valued for use in constructing items that need to be very strong.

Fir

Fir trees are tall and slender evergreens with needles and cones that resemble those of pines. They represent unity, family, and kindness, often being used as Christmas trees.

Hawthorn

Hawthorn is a shrub or small tree also known as hawberry and Mayflower. It symbolizes love and protection, and its berries have been used in love spells and marriage ceremonies. The dried fruits of hawthorn have medicinal properties, being used in some places around the world as a digestive aid.

Oak

Oak trees were considered sacred by the Celtic people since their size and longevity lent them to be a constant presence within a community, even as generation after generation of people passed on. It has a solid, sturdy, dense wood that can be used in many construction projects, especially as building frames and support beams. The traits associated with it are strength, longevity, stability, endurance, honesty, power, and justice.

Pine

Pine is an evergreen tree with fragrant needles and pine cones. It represents fertility, regeneration, and immortality. Their wood is the most commonly used type of timber for commercial purposes.

Rowan

Rowan is also known as mountain ash and has a dense wood perfect for carving sculptures and other works of art. It symbolizes wisdom, knowledge, and protection, and the Celtic people believed it could be used to ward off evil spirits and malevolent forces. Druids view rowan as a threshold between the physical world and the Otherworld.

Silver Fir

Silver fir is a tall, evergreen coniferous tree with a surprisingly strong, lightweight, even-textured wood with a fine grain. It is typically used in constructing furniture and paper, while its oil is present in perfumes and other aromatic products. The traits associated with it include hope, courage, and good fortune.

Willow

Willow trees have elongated leaves that hang down from their branches and can often be seen swaying in the wind. They symbolize adaptability, flexibility, and healing. Interestingly, chewing on the bark of a willow tree is believed to offer some relief from pain.

Yew

Yew is a coniferous tree that grows slowly but lives a very long time. It is associated with the Winter Solstice, death, and rebirth. The ancient Celtic people used the wood from yew trees to make a wide variety of weapons, tools, and other objects.

Chapter 9: Celtic Spells and Charms

Celtic magic is a tradition that goes back as far as the culture itself. Shamans and Druids both practiced forms of magic, and it was not uncommon for certain community members who had an affinity for spells and charms to take up the role of a local witch. Unlike the modern depictions of such people, most users of magic in the ancient Celtic society were viewed as wise, and their assistance with advice and abilities as healers made them valued members of the community. While much of the actual magic practiced by the ancient Celts has been lost to time, bits and pieces have been preserved by families who possess their own Book of Shadows.

Most Books of Shadows are unique, as the owners curate the specific collection of texts within it.
https://pixabay.com/es/photos/libro-naturaleza-sombra-leyendo-2669150/

Book of Shadows

The Book of Shadows is a corpus found within neopagan religions that contains religious texts and instructions on performing magical spells, charms, and rituals. It is traditionally passed down from one generation to the next within the same family, making it akin to the custom of a family Bible kept by many Christians. Most Books of Shadows are unique, as the specific collection of texts within it is curated by the owners, adding additional pieces to it as they learn new spells, charms, and rituals. Some families will also include personal writings that shine a light on their own journey through life as a neopagan practitioner.

One thing to remember about neopagan magic is the "Rule of Three," or the "Threefold Law." This asserts that any energy you put out in the world will return to you threefold, or three times as much as you put out. The intent of magical spells, charms, and rituals is to put out positive energy, so the positive energy that returns to you will be magnified by three. You must never attempt to use magic that puts out negative energy. Whatever short-term benefits it might grant you, the negative energy that returns will cause consequences that far outweigh whatever you might have gained.

Celtic Spells

Here is a list of different spells you can try on your own:

Spell for Good Fortune

This spell is meant to provide you with good luck. You will need the following:

- A candle
- String
- A trinket

Light the candle, then loop the string through the trinket and tie it. Start swinging the trinket above the flame and chant:

"A candle flickers, this trinket I pass, good energy and fortune come to me, wealth, knowledge, influence, energy. By good means come to me, wealth, knowledge, influence, energy. This trinket I pass into power, to attract to me wealth, knowledge, influence, energy, come to me!"

Repeat this three times, then wear the "necklace" around your neck. The more you do this, the more powerful the effect will be."

Beauty Spell

This spell is meant to increase your attractiveness. You will need the following:

- A mirror

- A camera

- A candle

To cast it, you must do the following:

During a full moon, take a mirror and go outside. If you can't go outside, just open a window and ensure the moon is reflected in the mirror.

Take a picture of your hair, lips, eyes, or whatever you want to change, and place it on the mirror.

While concentrating on it, say, *"Moonshine, Starlight, let the wind carry your light. Let your glow cover my body, and let your shine cover every eye."*

Once you are done, dispose of the picture by burning it with a candle. Repeat these steps to improve the effects of the spell."

Dragon's Blood Peace Spell

This spell is meant to keep the peace within your home. You will need the following:

- A glass bottle, flask, or vial

- Red, flexible sealing wax

- Matches or a lighter

- Sugar

- Salt

- Dragon's Blood Powder (a powdered form of a resin extracted from the fruit of the Calamus Draco tree)

First, *mix together the ingredients, adding 1 part sugar, 1 part salt, and 1 part Dragon's blood.*

Seal the bottle, flask, or vial with the red wax.

Recite the following spell: "I call upon the Mother of Earth to grant me peace.

I ask you to bless this home with serenity.

Let clear minds overcome angry hearts.

Let gentleness and kindness infuse this space."

Place the sealed container in a shared space around your home where your family spends a significant amount of time, such as the kitchen or a living room. This spell will give off a calming energy and keep the peace between your family members."

Celtic Charms

Here's a list of charms you can try on your own:

Protection Charm

A standard protection charm will create a field of energy surrounding your chosen space. The larger the area, the more energy is needed to keep them active. To cast this charm, you will need the following:

- 3-5 candles
- A doll or effigy
- Chamomile petals
- Pen and paper
- Matches or lighter
- Flame-resistant bowl or ashtray

Starting off, write the following down on the piece of paper, "Please protect this space from all harm. I trust in the power of the gods and goddesses, and I will not allow negative energy to invade my space. Once this charm has been cast, it will protect this space for three times three days."

When you have finished writing, fold the paper up and place it in the bowl or ashtray. Now you must set the candles up around the perimeter of the area that you wish to protect. This can be in the shape of a triangle, square, rectangle, circle, or five-point star.

After you set the candle down, light it and say the following: *"I light this flame to ward off any evil that seeks to invade my space. So long as it burns, no darkness will seep through its barrier."*

Repeat this for each candle, and then return to the bowl with the paper in it. Place the doll or effigy in front of it. This will represent the power of the charm, as you will channel the protective energy into it. Sprinkle the chamomile petals into the bowl over it, and then set the paper aflame.

As it burns, focus on visualizing a protective layer of energy surrounding your chosen area. Hold your doll or effigy in your hand when the flames have died down and speak these words: "This power now protects my space from all harm. *I have nothing to fear from anything outside it. Thank you for delivering me from the darkness and into the light.*"

It is now safe to snuff out the candles, as the protection charm is fueled by the energy you put into the doll or effigy. It must remain within the protected area in order to work. Taking it beyond the perimeter you've established will cause it to lose its effect and leave you vulnerable to harm. After nine days, you can burn or bury the doll or effigy, as its power has been spent. You can repeat the charm ritual if you desire to maintain the protection magic keeping you safe."

Charm against Depression

Depression is sometimes known as a "Fairy Blast," as the ancient Celts believed that when a person fell into a listless, unenergetic, emotionally-numb state, they were no longer themselves. A fairy was said to have been the culprit, and a Fairy Doctor was brought in to counter the negative effects of the Fairy Blast. You can cast the same charm that they did to rid the afflicted person of the Fairy Blast. To do this, you will need the following:

- Blessed water
- A basin
- Fire (a candle or hearth)
- Incense sticks

Before you begin, light the candle or hearth. You first need to pour the blessed water over the person's hands, catching it in the basin.

As you do this, say: *"In the name of Lugh, who shows strength before the gods and stands among them, lend me your shining sword so that I might rid this poor soul of their afflictions."*

Be careful to avoid letting the water get sullied. Next, light the incense sticks and hold them in front of the person. Allow them to burn for several minutes, infusing the air with its protective energy.

Once you have finished burning the sticks, say: *"Cast off this veil and return this person to me. Begone, fairies! I know you for what you are. Begone from this place!"*

Place the candle and incense sticks into the basin with the water to put them out, or toss the water over the fire in your hearth. This charm will help ward off any further symptoms of depression."

Creating Your Own Book of Shadows

You can create your own Book of Shadows by copying these spells and charms with handwriting onto a piece of paper. Do not just print them off, as the texts within your Book of Shadows should all have a personal touch. Add in any notes from your experience with attempting the spells and charms. You can also write up a brief summary of what first got you interested in Celtic magic and the first steps you took to learn about it. Although your Book of Shadows will be relatively thin initially, as you add more to it over the years, you will gather an impressive amount of knowledge that you can then pass on to the next generation in your family.

Chapter 10: Celtic Holidays and Festivals

Many Celtic holidays and festivals throughout the calendar year celebrate various aspects of Celtic society. The main festivals are those from the Wheel of the Year. Still, plenty of minor holidays focus on more niche subjects, such as a feast dedicated to a single deity or a seasonal occasion. The Celtic people loved to celebrate. Their festivals often included singing, dancing, music, games, feasts, bonfires, rituals, and dedications to the gods.

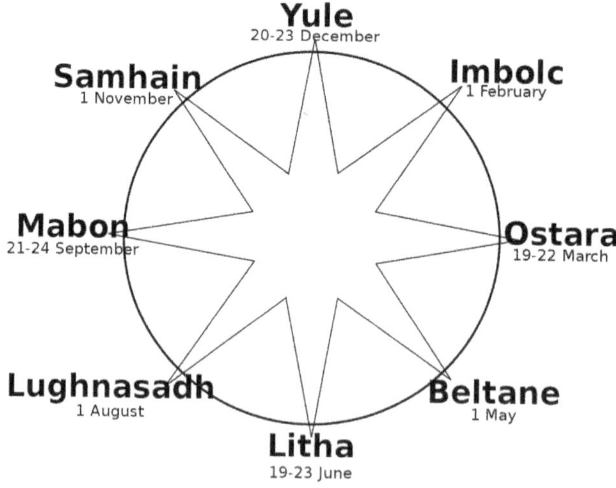

Many Celtic holidays and festivals throughout the calendar year celebrate various aspects of Celtic society.

https://commons.wikimedia.org/wiki/File:Wheel_of_the_Year.svg

The Wheel of the Year

The Wheel of the Year is a cycle of eight annual seasonal festivals that coincide with major solar events, such as the solstices and equinoxes and the midpoints between them. These eight festivals can be laid out around the Wheel of the Year, turning it as the seasons come and go, with the current solar event or midpoint sitting at the top. Just as each calendar year involves a cycle of seasons associated with birth, growth, maturity, death, and rebirth, all things within the world experience a similar cycle.

Imbolc

Imbolc is the festival celebrated halfway between the winter solstice and the vernal equinox. It marks the beginning of spring when the land is going through the birth and rebirth part of the cycle. This is when seeds are starting to be sown, and spring cleaning is a common tradition. The Celtic people would visit holy wells, praying for good health. They would recite these prayers while walking "sunwise," or clockwise, around the well. Offerings of coins or "clooties" were often left for the gods, and water drawn from the wells was used in cleansings and blessings of the home, livestock, crop fields, and loved ones.

The Celtic pagans dedicated Imbolc to the goddess Brigid, syncretized with St. Brigid by the Christian Church, adopting this festival as St. Brigid's Day. People would leave strips of cloth or clothing outside, hoping that St. Brigid would bless them. Christians also celebrate this day as Candlemas, which commemorates the presentation of Jesus at the Temple. Imbolc is the first of the three spring festivals. In Wales, this festival is called "Gŵyl Fair y Canhwyllau," which translates to "Mary's Festival of the Candles."

Ostara

Ostara is a festival that falls on the vernal equinox. This day has roughly the same amount of day and night, balancing darkness and light. However, it marks the point when day will start to overtake night, with light on the rise. Nature is in full bloom, with many plants flowering and new animals entering their major growth stage. The Christian liturgical calendar uses the vernal equinox to determine when Easter will be celebrated yearly since it is a moveable feast with no set date. Ostara is the second of the three spring festivals. In Wales, this festival is called "Alban Eilir," which translates to "Equinox of the Spring."

Beltane

Beltane is the festival celebrated halfway between the vernal equinox and summer solstice. It marks the end of spring and the beginning of summer when the land is going through the growth part of the cycle. It is also known as May Day, and maypoles are a popular tradition for the Celtic people and the cultures descended from them. Bonfires are another typical activity for celebrating this festival. In the past, sacrifices occurred alongside the bonfires, but these practices have been phased out by the neopagans and modern cultures.

Certain traditions, such as warding off or appeasing the fairies in an effort to protect crops and livestock, are still practiced today. Like with Imbolc, holy wells are visited, moving sunwise around them, and similar offerings are left to receive a blessing from the gods. Traditional foods are prepared, and feasts are given for families and communities to celebrate together, sharing in one's good fortune and asking for blessings and protection during the oncoming season. Beltane is the third of the three spring festivals. In Wales, this festival is called "Calan Haf," which translates to "First Day of Summer."

Litha

Litha is the festival that falls on the summer solstice, the longest day of the year, and as the midpoint of the season, it is also known as Midsummer. Nature is at the peak of its maturation, reaching the end of the growth part of the cycle. Much of this festival consists of venerating the sun, giving it thanks for its nourishing light, and asking the gods to protect their crops and livestock until the harvest season. Some celebrations go on late into the night, with candles and bonfires preserving the light through the shortest period of darkness for the year. Dancing, singing, feasting, and other revelries often occur during this holiday. Litha is the only summer festival. In Wales, this festival is called "Alban Hefin," which translates to "Solstice of the Summer."

Lughnasadh

Lughnasadh is the festival celebrated halfway between the summer solstice and the autumnal equinox. It marks the start of the harvest season, as well as the end of summer and the beginning of autumn. One of the most popular traditions during this festival is baking bread using the first grains harvested that year. Some people also bake a small figure representing the god Lugh into their bread, believing this will ensure a bountiful harvest that season.

Christianity syncretized their harvest festival with Lughnasadh, known as Lammas, or the Loaf Mass Day. Their customs are similar to that of the pagan holiday, including baking bread with the first harvested grains. However, rather than offerings to the pagan gods, Christians give thanks and pray to the Abrahamic God and Jesus Christ. They also celebrate the feast of St. Alphonsus Liguori on this day, which coincides with the date of his death. Lughnasadh is the first of the three autumn or harvest festivals. In Wales, this festival is called "Calan Awst," which translates to "First Day of August."

Mabon

Mabon is the festival that falls on the autumnal equinox. This day has roughly the same amount of night and day, balancing darkness and light. However, it marks the point when night will start to overtake day, with darkness on the rise. This is when crops have reached their full maturity and are waiting to be reaped. Neopagans perform a thanksgiving ritual, showing gratitude for the fruits yielded by the earth and recognizing their duty to share their good fortune with others. They also seek to gain the gods' blessing for the oncoming winter. Mabon is the second of the autumn or harvest festivals. Its name is actually derived from the figure of Mabon ap Modron in Welsh mythology, but it is also known in Wales as "Alban Elfed," which translates to "Equinox of the Autumn."

Samhain

Samhain is the festival celebrated halfway between the autumnal equinox and winter solstice. It marks the end of summer and the beginning of winter – when the land is going through the death part of the cycle. The name Samhain is Gaelic for "Summer's End." The harvest season ends when the crops have yielded up the last of their bounty. The Celtic people would have bonfires and perform divination rituals during this time, as it was customary to honor the dead and appease the spirits. It was believed that the veil between the physical world and the spiritual realm was at its weakest during Samhain, allowing the spirits to walk the Earth for the duration of the festival.

There was a popular tradition known as *mumming and guising,* where people dressed in costume or disguise, wearing masks or painting their faces. The idea was that they would be impersonating the spirits and souls of the dead, protecting them from harm by blending in with these supernatural entities. They went door to door, singing songs and reciting verses in exchange for food or treats. The mummers would threaten that they would do mischief to the residents if they were not compensated for their efforts.

The practice of mumming and guising is very similar to the modern custom of "trick or treating," where people (usually children) dress up in costumes and visit houses to get candy or treats. The name of the activity harkens back to the older Celtic tradition, where the rhetorical choice of a "trick" or a "treat" is similar to the threat of doing mischief if the mummer was not given food. Trick or treating normally takes place on Halloween, or All Hallows' Eve, which is the eve of the Christian holiday known as All Hallows' Day or All Saints' Day. This is another instance of syncretization, with the Christian Church adopting Samhain and some of its traditions for their own holiday. Samhain is the third of the autumn or harvest festivals. In Wales, this festival is called "Nos Calan Gaeaf," which translates to "Eve of the First Day of Winter."

Yule

Yule is the festival that falls on the winter solstice. This is the shortest day of the year, and as it is the midpoint of the winter season, it is also called Midwinter. Nature is at the nadir of the death part of the cycle but preparing to enter the rebirth part. Christianity syncretized Yule with their midwinter holidays, resulting in the liturgical season known as Christmastide. Gift-giving and feasting are popular customs for this festival, as well as having gatherings of friends and family. A Yule log is traditionally chosen and burnt in the hearth, and the warmth and light are meant to protect the home from the harsh, wintry conditions outside. Yule is the only winter festival. In Wales, this festival is called "Alban Arthan," which translates to "Solstice of the Little Bear," a name that refers to the Welsh myths of King Arthur.

Appendix: Glossary of Gaelic Terms

Celt/Celtic: A collection of Indo-European people connected by their shared cultural experiences and languages.

Gael/Gaelic: The native peoples from Ireland, Scotland, and the Isle of Man. They speak a branch of the Celtic languages known as Gaelic (Irish), Scottish Gaelic, and Manx.

Shaman: A religious figure who can access the spiritual realm and influence good and evil spirits. They enter a trance-like state during rituals and ceremonies and practice healing and divination.

Druid: A high-ranking member within ancient Celtic society who served as a religious leader, keeper of lore; also, legal authorities, adjudicators, healers, and political advisors. Modern Druids serve a similar function, although they now mostly focus on the religious, historical, and healing aspects of their role.

Spiritual Realm: Also known as the Spirit Realm, it is a hidden world that exists alongside the physical world but is unable to be accessed by most people. This is where many spirits dwell, and shamans are proficient in communicating with spirits across the veil and entering the spiritual realm through ritualistic means.

Otherworld: A realm of deities and supernatural beings that features heavily in Celtic, Irish, and Welsh mythology. It is also where the souls of the dead go after their physical body perishes.

Soul: The immaterial essence and energy of a human being that exists separate from their physical body.

Spirit: The soul of a person, animal, or other creature, as well as certain supernatural beings that lack a physical body.

Animism: The belief that plants, inanimate objects, and other natural phenomena have a living spirit.

Entheogens: Any chemical substance, usually coming from an organic source, which can be ingested to produce an altered state of consciousness for religious or spiritual purposes. Shamans normally use these to enter a trance in order to commune with spirits or enter the spiritual realm.

Ogham: An ancient Celtic alphabet consisting of 25 (originally 20) characters that are formed by parallel tally marks, dashes, dots, or other basic shapes in various configurations across a continuous line.

Tree Astrology: A practice of predicting a person's personality and specific traits based on their date of birth and when during a season this occurred. Each category is based on the movement of the moon coordinated with a lunar calendar that results in 13 signs instead of the 12 in the zodiac.

Awen: A concept from Welsh mythology defined as a creative energy that inspires poets, bards, and other artists. It can also be the personification of a muse for creative artists in general.

The Wheel of the Year: The annual cycle of seasonal festivals, consisting of the year's primary solar events (the solstices and equinoxes) and the midpoints between them.

Imbolc: The festival is halfway between the winter solstice and the vernal equinox that marks the beginning of spring and is also known as Candlemas.

Ostara: The festival that falls on the vernal equinox when there is a balance between darkness and light, with light on the rise.

Beltane: The festival is halfway between the vernal equinox and summer solstice that marks the beginning of summer, and is also known as May Day.

Litha: The festival that falls on the summer solstice, also known as Midsummer, is the longest day of the year.

Lughnasadh: The festival is halfway between the summer solstice and the autumnal equinox; it marks the start of the harvest season and is also known as Lammas.

Mabon: The festival that falls on the autumnal equinox when there is a balance between light and darkness, with darkness on the rise.

Samhain: The festival is halfway between the autumnal equinox and winter solstice, marking the end of the harvest season, and is also known as Halloween.

Yule: The festival that falls on the winter solstice, also known as Christmastide, is the shortest day of the year.

Here's another book by Silvia Hill that you might like

Free Bonus from Silvia Hill available for limited time

Hi Spirituality Lovers!

My name is Silvia Hill, and first off, I want to THANK YOU for reading my book.

Now you have a chance to join my exclusive spirituality email list so you can get the ebooks below for free as well as the potential to get more spirituality ebooks for free! Simply click the link below to join.

P.S. Remember that it's 100% free to join the list.

Bibliography

What is Paganism? (2011, December 17). Pagan Federation International. https://www.paganfederation.org/what-is-paganism/

Hertzenberg, S., & Hertzenberg, S. (n.d.). What Are the Different Pagan Religions? Beliefnet.Com. https://www.beliefnet.com/faiths/pagan-and-earth-based/what-are-the-different-pagan-religions.aspx

Buker, R. (2018). Samhain. Piscataqua Press.

Celebrating the ancient Egyptian new year. (n.d.). Gov.Eg. https://egymonuments.gov.eg/events/celebrating-the-ancient-egyptian-new-year/

Colagrossi, M. (2018, November 27). 10 of the greatest ancient and pagan holidays. Big Think. https://bigthink.com/the-past/pagan-holidays/

Dowdey, S. (2007, December 5). How reincarnation works. HowStuffWorks. https://people.howstuffworks.com/reincarnation.htm

EarthSpirit. (2017, April 14). Paganism and Myths of Creation. EarthSpirit; EarthSpirit Inc. http://www.earthspirit.com/paganism-myths-creation

Kershaw, D. (2022, June 8). Pagan gods from across the ancient world. History Cooperative; The History Cooperative. https://historycooperative.org/pagan-gods/

Land, G. (n.d.). The 12 gods and goddesses of pagan Rome. History Hit. https://www.historyhit.com/the-gods-and-goddesses-of-pagan-rome/

Mark, J. J. (2016). Egyptian afterlife - the field of reeds. World History Encyclopedia. https://www.worldhistory.org/article/877/egyptian-afterlife---the-field-of-reeds/

Pagan beliefs. (n.d.). https://www.bbc.co.uk/religion/religions/paganism/beliefs/beliefs.shtml

Paganism. (n.d.). Nhs.uk. http://www.waht.nhs.uk/en-GB/NHS-Mobile/Our-Services/?depth=4&srcid=2007

Ravenwood, C. (2021). Celebrating samhain: A coloring and activity book. Independently Published.

S., J. (2019, June 3). Norse afterlife. Norse and Viking Mythology; vkngjewelry. https://blog.vkngjewelry.com/en/norse-afterlife/

Sogani, G. (2022, February 6). Religion and gods in the ancient pagan world. Wondrium Daily. https://www.wondriumdaily.com/religion-and-gods-in-the-ancient-pagan-world/

The Current Chief, The Former Chief, & Patroness, O. (2019, December 15). Samhain - rituals & traditions. Order of Bards, Ovates & Druids; OBOD. https://druidry.org/druid-way/teaching-and-practice/druid-festivals/samhain-festival

The Hell of ancient Egypt. (n.d.). Touregypt.net. http://www.touregypt.net/featurestories/hell.htm

Tomlin, A. (2022, May 18). Norse gods, goddesses and giants: the ultimate list. Routes North. https://www.routesnorth.com/language-and-culture/norse-gods-goddesses-and-giants/

What is Yule? (n.d.). Almanac.com. https://www.almanac.com/content/what-yule-log-christmas-traditions

Wigington, P. (2013, March 25). What do Pagans believe about the creation of the world? Learn Religions. https://www.learnreligions.com/pagans-and-creation-stories-2561497

Wigington, P. (2019, March 28). Norse deities. Learn Religions. https://www.learnreligions.com/norse-deities-4590158

John Halstead, C. (2015, October 2). We're Not All Witches: An Introduction to Neo-Paganism. HuffPost

Magick, B. B. (2018, December 13). Witchcraft, Wicca, and Paganism - What's the Difference? Blessed Be Magick. https://blessedbemagick.com/blogs/news/witchcraft-wicca-and-paganism-what-s-the-difference

Stonestreet, J., Leander, K., & Rivera, R. (2020, February 4). Wicca and Eclectic Neo-Paganism: Beliefs and Practices, Emerging Worldviews 22. Breakpoint. https://ec2-52-34-39-89.us-west-2.compute.amazonaws.com/wicca-and-eclectic-neo-paganism-beliefs-and-practices-emerging-worldviews-22/

Bradley, C. (2020, December 23). "Pagan" vs. "Wicca": What Is The Difference? Dictionary.Com. https://www.dictionary.com/e/pagan-vs-wicca-pagan-vs-heathen/

We'Moon. (n.d.). Understanding Altars: What is an altar, and how to bring altar magic into my life. We'Moon. https://wemoon.ws/blogs/magical-arts/understanding-altars-what-is-an-altar-and-how-to-bring-altar-magic-into-my-life

Wigington, P. (n.d.). 9 Things to Include in Your Book of Shadows. Learn Religions. https://www.learnreligions.com/make-a-book-of-shadows-2562826

Blake, D. (2021, September 16). 10 Easy Ways to Create a Book of Shadows or Make an Existing Book Your Own. Llewellyn Worldwide. https://www.llewellyn.com/journal/article/2942

Vamvoukakis, A. (2022, July 11). How to Cast a Circle for Wiccans and Witches. The Embroidered Forest.

Chatterjee, A. (2021, October 30). Be a modern witch with 7 daily spells and rituals that attract positivity. Tweak India. https://tweakindia.com/culture/discover/modern-witch-share-7-daily-practices-to-attract-good-vibes-only/

Siedlak, M. J. (2016). Wiccan Spells: Mojo's Wiccan Series. Createspace Independent Publishing Platform.

Dan. (2012, November 14). Norse mythology for Smart People - the ultimate online guide to Norse mythology and religion. Norse Mythology for Smart People. https://norse-mythology.org/

Norman. (2009, February 14). The origins of the Norse mythology. The Norse Gods; Norman. https://thenorsegods.com/the-origins-of-the-norse-mythology/

The faith. (n.d.). Asatru UK. https://www.asatruuk.org/the-faith

The old Nordic religion today. (n.d.). National Museum of Denmark. https://en.natmus.dk/historical-knowledge/denmark/prehistoric-period-until-1050-ad/the-viking-age/religion-magic-death-and-rituals/the-old-nordic-religion-today/

Time Nomads. (2021, June 20). Norse Paganism for beginners: Quick introduction + resources. Time Nomads | Your Pagan Store Online; Time Nomads. https://www.timenomads.com/norse-paganism-for-beginners/

Wigington, P. (2019, March 28). Norse deities. Learn Religions. https://www.learnreligions.com/norse-deities-4590158

Aletheia. (2018, October 22). How to induce a trance state for deep psychospiritual work ★ LonerWolf. LonerWolf.

Dan. (2012, November 15). Seidr. Norse Mythology for Smart People. https://norse-mythology.org/concepts/seidr/

Greenberg, M. (2020, November 16). Seidr magic in viking culture. MythologySource; Mike Greenberg, PhD. https://mythologysource.com/seidr-magic-viking-culture/

Skjalden. (2018, March 11). Völva the viking witch or seeress. Nordic Culture. https://skjalden.com/volva-the-viking-witch-or-seeress/

Wright, M. S. (2015, March 3). Wicca for beginners: Visualizations for grounding and centering meditations. Exemplore. https://exemplore.com/wicca-witchcraft/Wicca-for-Beginners-Visualizations-for-Grounding-and-Centering-Meditations

Dan. (2012, November 14). Runes. Norse Mythology for Smart People. https://norse-mythology.org/runes/

Anne C. Sørensen, R. M. J. H. (n.d.). Runes. Vikingeskibsmuseet i Roskilde. https://www.vikingeskibsmuseet.dk/en/professions/education/viking-age-people/runes

Dan. (2013, June 29). The Origins of the Runes. Norse Mythology for Smart People. https://norse-mythology.org/runes/the-origins-of-the-runes/

Dan. (2013, June 29). Runic Philosophy and Magic. Norse Mythology for Smart People. https://norse-mythology.org/runes/runic-philosophy-and-magic/

Dan. (2013, June 29). The Meanings of the Runes. Norse Mythology for Smart People. https://norse-mythology.org/runes/the-meanings-of-the-runes/

Shelley, A. (2022, February 22). Futhark Runes: Symbols, Meanings and How to Use Them. Andrea Shelley Designs. https://andreashelley.com/blog/futhark-runes-symbols-and-meanings/

Sam, T. +., & Wander, T. (2020, November 25). Rune Meanings And How To Use Rune Stones For Divination —. Two Wander x Elysium Rituals. https://www.twowander.com/blog/rune-meanings-how-to-use-runestones-for-divination

Sam, T. +., & Wander, T. (2020, November 25). Rune Meanings And How To Use Rune Stones For Divination —. Two Wander x Elysium Rituals. https://www.twowander.com/blog/rune-meanings-how-to-use-runestones-for-divination

AstroMundus, & Happy, happy.com. pt. (2021, November 18). Runes and Their Meanings •. AstroMundus. https://astromundus.com/en/runes-meanings/

Wigington, P. (n.d.). What Is Rune Casting? Origins and Techniques. Learn Religions. https://www.learnreligions.com/rune-casting-4783609

Jessica, S. (2021, April 27). How to Read Rune Stones. Norse and Viking Mythology. https://blog.vkngjewelry.com/en/rune-divination-how-to-read-the-runes/

I. E. (IrishMyths.com). (2022, April 12). Who were the druids? Demystifying the mystics of the ancient Celtic world. Irish Myths. https://irishmyths.com/2022/04/11/what-are-druids/

Spaeth, M. J. D. (2020). Celtic Shamanism. In Encyclopedia of Psychology and Religion (pp. 370–372). Springer International Publishing.

Terravara. (2021, April 23). Shamanism vs druidism: What's the difference? Terravara. https://www.terravara.com/shamanism-vs-druidism/

The Current Chief, The Former Chief, & Patroness, O. (2019a, November 27). Bard. Order of Bards, Ovates & Druids; OBOD. https://druidry.org/druid-way/what-druidry/what-is-a-bard

The Current Chief, The Former Chief, & Patroness, O. (2019b, November 27). Ovate. Order of Bards, Ovates & Druids; OBOD. https://druidry.org/druid-way/what-druidry/what-is-an-ovate

The Current Chief, The Former Chief, & Patroness, O. (2019c, November 27). What is druidry ? Order of Bards, Ovates & Druids; OBOD. https://druidry.org/druid-way/what-druidry

The Editors of Encyclopedia Britannica. (2022). Druid. In Encyclopedia Britannica.

The sacred fire - Celtic shamanism. (n.d.). Sacredfire.net. https://www.sacredfire.net/shaman.html

Who were the Druids? (2017, March 21). Historic UK. https://www.historic-uk.com/HistoryUK/HistoryofWales/Druids/

Wigington, P. (2007, May 23). Who are today's Druids? Learn Religions. https://www.learnreligions.com/about-druidism-druidry-2562546

An Introduction to the Basics of Modern Druid practice. (2017, January 29). The Druid Network. https://druidnetwork.org/what-is-druidry/learning-resources/shaping-the-wheel/introduction-basics-modern-druid-practice/

Damh the Bard. (2015, July 24). Druidry for beginners - where to start? The senses. Damh the Bard. https://www.paganmusic.co.uk/druidry-for-beginners-where-to-start-the-senses/

Ede-Weaving, M. (2021, April 22). Awen. Order of Bards, Ovates & Druids. https://druidry.org/resources/awen

How does one become a Druid? (2013, March 10). The Druid Network. https://druidnetwork.org/what-is-druidry/beliefs-and-definitions/articles/how-does-one-become-a-druid/

Hertzenberg, S., & Hertzenberg, S. (n.d.). What Are the Different Pagan Religions? Beliefnet.Com. https://www.beliefnet.com/faiths/pagan-and-earth-based/what-are-the-different-pagan-religions.aspx

Pagan paths. (n.d.). https://www.bbc.co.uk/religion/religions/paganism/subdivisions/paths.shtml

Berry, L. A. (2022, August 25). Who were the Druids? A history of Druidism in Britain. British Heritage. https://britishheritage.com/history/history-Druids-britain

Burrows, G. (2020). Portico: The near future thriller that will keep you guessing. Gideon Burrows.

https://access.portico.org/Portico/auView?auId=ark:%2F27927%2Fphzjqstqh

Caesar, G. J. (2017). Bellum Gallicum (J. H. Schmalz, Ed.). de Gruyter Mouton.

Carney, J. (1975). The Invention of the Ogam Cipher. Ériu, 22, 62–63.

Cox, R. A. V. (1999). The language of the ogam inscriptions of Scotland. An Clo Gaidhealach.

Cross, T. P., & Slover, C. H. (1995). Ancient Irish tales: The ulster cycle. Four Courts Press.

Curriculum Development Unit. (1982). Heroic tales from the ulster cycle (2nd ed.). O'Brien Press.

Dan. (2012, November 15). Shamanism. Norse Mythology for Smart People. https://norse-mythology.org/concepts/shamanism/

Davis, R. E., Peterson, K. E., Rothschild, S. K., & Resnicow, K. (2011). Pushing the envelope for cultural appropriateness: does evidence support cultural tailoring in type 2 diabetes interventions for Mexican American adults? The Diabetes Educator, 37(2), 227–238. https://doi.org/10.1177/0145721710395329

Eickhoff, R. L. (2004). The Red Branch tales: The sixth book in the ulster cycle. Forge.

Fhearaigh, C., & Stampton, T. (1998). Ogham: An Irish alphabet. Hippocrene Books.

Glosecki, S. O. (1988). Wolf of the bees: Germanic shamanism and the bear hero. Journal of Ritual Studies, 2(1), 31–53. http://www.jstor.org/stable/44368362

Harris, K. (n.d.). Mythology: Oak trees and why people worshiped them. History Daily. https://historydaily.org/tree-gods-worshiping-mighty-oak-trees/8

Info. (2020a, February 11). A re-evaluation of the ogham tree list. Order of Bards, Ovates & Druids. https://Druidry.org/resources/a-re-evaluation-of-the-ogham-tree-list

Info. (2020b, February 11). Anglo-Celtic medicine ways - the shamanism of pre-Christian Britain. Order of Bards, Ovates & Druids. https://Druidry.org/resources/anglo-celtic-medicine-ways-the-shamanism-of-pre-christian-britain

Jackson, K. (1948). A Grammar of Old Irish. R. Thurneysen, D. A. Binchy, Osborn Bergin. Speculum, 23(2), 335–339. https://doi.org/10.2307/2852977

Loh-Hagan, V. (2020). Celtic tree astrology. 45th Parallel Press.

MacManus, S. (1988). Rocky road to Dublin. Moytura Press.

MacNeill, E. (1931). Archaisms in the Ogham Inscriptions. Hodges Figgis.

Martin, G. R. R. (2011). Song of ice and fire set: A game of thrones, a clash of kings, a storm of swords, a feast for crows, a dance with dragons. Zatpix Re-Packaged Edition.

Miller, M. (2012). Ogham - the magical Celtic tree alphabet (2nd ed.). Ogma Publications.

Moss, V. (1985). Beating the stress connection. Self-hypnosis. AORN Journal, 41(4), 720–722.

Ogham translator - online ogam writing converter. (n.d.). Dcode.Fr https://www.dcode.fr/ogham-alphabet

O'Hara, K. (2022, January 10). 15 Celtic symbols and meanings (an Irishman's 2022 guide). The Irish Road Trip. https://www.theirishroadtrip.com/celtic-symbols-and-meanings/

Padilla, R., Gomez, V., Biggerstaff, S. L., & Mehler, P. S. (2001). Use of curanderismo in a public health care system. Archives of Internal Medicine, 161(10), 1336–1340. https://doi.org/10.1001/archinte.161.10.1336

Piattelli-Palmarini, M. (2000). Tower of babel. Trends in Ecology & Evolution, 15(4), 173–174. https://doi.org/10.1016/s0169-5347(99)01804-2

Reyes-Ortiz, C. A., Rodriguez, M., & Markides, K. S. (2009). The role of spirituality healing with perceptions of the medical encounter among Latinos. Journal of General Internal Medicine, 24 Suppl 3(S3), 542–547. https://doi.org/10.1007/s11606-009-1067-9

Ryan, C. (2012). Border states in the work of Tom Mac Intyre: A Paleo-postmodern perspective. Cambridge Scholars Publishing.

Salter, A. (1941). Three Techniques of Autohypnosis. The Journal of General Psychology, 24(2), 423–438. https://doi.org/10.1080/00221309.1941.10544386

Sinn, S. (2011, July 13). Muin (grape vine). Living Library. https://livinglibraryblog.com/muin-grape/

Skjalden. (2018, March 11). Völva the viking witch or seeress. Nordic Culture. https://skjalden.com/volva-the-viking-witch-or-seeress/

Sleath, B. L., & Williams, J. W., Jr. (2004). Hispanic ethnicity, language, and depression: physician-patient communication and patient use of alternative treatments. International Journal of Psychiatry in Medicine, 34(3), 235–246. https://doi.org/10.2190/VQU1-QYWT-XW6Y-4M14

Spence, L. (2005). Celtic spells and charms. Kessinger Publishing.

Spilsbury, L. (2017). The Mayas. Raintree.

Stewart Macalister, R. A. (2014). The secret languages of Ireland. Cambridge University Press.

Terravara. (2021, April 23). Shamanism vs Druidism: What's the difference? Terravara. https://www.terravara.com/shamanism-vs-Druidism/

The origins of shamanism. (n.d.). Gaia. https://www.gaia.com/article/how-much-do-you-know-about-shamanism

Walsh, J. K. (2017). Tezcatlipoca, the Smoking Mirror. Createspace Independent Publishing Platform.

Williams, B. (1996). The Roman conquest of Britain. Heinemann Library.

Williams, T. W. (2013). In quest of life; Or, the revelations of the wiyatatao of xipantl. The last high priest of the Aztecs. Theclassics